THE COMPLETE MEDITERRANEAN DIET COOKBOOK

THE ULITIMATE QUICK AND ESY GUIDE ON HOW TO EFFECTIVELY LOSE WEIGHT FAST, DELICIOUS RECIPES THAT BEGINNERS AND BUSY PEOPLE CAN DO

SANDRA RAMOS

Copyright - 2021 - All rights reserved.

The content contained within this book may not be reproduced, duplicated or transmitted without direct written permission from the author or the publisher.

Under no circumstances will any blame or legal responsibility be held against the publisher, or author, for any damages, reparation, or monetary loss due to the information contained within this book, either directly or indirectly.

Legal Notice:

This book is copyright protected. This book is only for personal use. You cannot amend, distribute, sell, use, quote or paraphrase any part, or the content within this book, without the consent of the author or publisher.

Disclaimer Notice:

Please note the information contained within this document is for educational and entertainment purposes only. All effort has been executed to present accurate, up to date, and reliable, complete information. No warranties of any kind are declared or implied.
Readers acknowledge that the author is not engaging in the rendering of legal, financial, medical or professional advice. The content within this book has been derived from various sources. Please consult a licensed professional before attempting any techniques outlined in this book.

By reading this document, the reader agrees that under no circumstances is the author responsible for any losses, direct or indirect, which are incurred as a result of the use of information contained within this document, including, but not limited to, - errors, omissions, or inaccuracies.

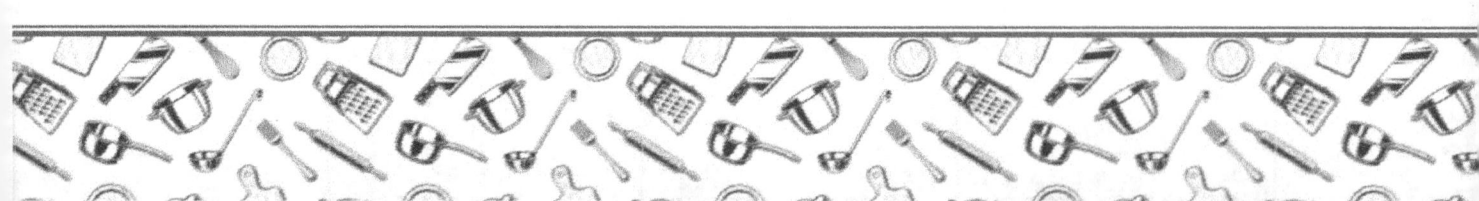

Table of Contents

INTRODUCTION 1

Chapter 1: Why this type of diet is the right for you? 5

Chapter 2: Your Mindset and this diet 9

Chapter 4: Exercise 15

Chapter 5: The recipes in this book 16

Breakfast Recipes 18

    Seafood Omelet 18

    Eggs with Sausages and Spinach 19

    Terrine for Breakfast 20

    Frittata with Asparagus and Onions 21

    Italian Cheese Toast 22

    Omelet with Spinach, Ham and Cheese 23

    Orange Pancakes 24

    Oatmeal Apricot Bites 25

    Olive oil and Onion Bread for Breakfast 26

    Scrambled Eggs 27

    Sandwiches with Almond Butter 28

    Western Frittata 29

    Scrambled Eggs from Greece 30

    Avocados Stuffed 31

    Spinach Pancakes 32

French Toast with Pecans 33

Oven Omelet with Pears 34

Omelet with Baby Spinach 35

Vegetable Poached Eggs 36

Italian Sandwich for Breakfast 37

Scalloped Eggs 38

Avocado and Egg Sandwich 39

Potato Pancakes 40

Tuna Melt Sandwich 41

Omelet from Apples 42

Curried Tuna Melt 43

Scrambled Eggs with Shrimps 44

Lunch Recipes 45

Chicken with Almonds and Oranges 45

Halibut with Salsa 46

Tomato Spinach and Bean Burrito 47

Steak Stuffed with Spinach 48

Spinach and Lentils 49

Sandwich with Mushrooms and Artichokes 50

Stuffed Mushrooms 51

Asparagus Wrapped in Salmon 52

Eggplant and Lamb Stew 53

Burgers with Portobello Mushrooms 54

Orange Beef and Beans 55

Chicken with Cranberry 56

Penne with Eggplant 57

Eggplant and Mushroom with Wild Rice 58

Eggplant Moussaka 59

Eggplant Balls 60

Asparagus Pasta 61

Chicken Burgers with Feta Cheese 62

Eggplant Burgers 63

Rice with Lemon and Spinach 64

Lemon, Parsley and Chicken Breast for Lunch 65

Black Bean and Artichoke Burritos 66

Sesame Vegetables with Rice 67

Syrian Style Lentil and Spinach Soup 68

Roasted Red Potatoes and Asparagus 69

Spinach and Rice (It can be used as Brunch) 70

Sweet Potatoes with Raisins and Pecans 71

Orange Couscous 72

Chicken with Almonds 73

Eggplant and Garlic Sauce 74

Dinner Recipes 75

Orange Lamb 75

Spinach and Turkey Lasagna 76

Steak and Potato Salad 77

Filled Tomatoes 78

Greek Lamb Roast 79

Keftedes 80

- Turkey with Pine and Chestnuts 81
- Stuffed Peppers 82
- Crab Cakes 83
- Lentil Soup 84
- Greek Tacos 85
- Mussels with Potatoes and Black Olives 86
- Skewers from Lemon and Chicken 87
- Spinach and Cherries with Goat Cheese 88
- Eggplant and Tomato Bake 89
- Mediterranean Veggie Chicken 90

30-day meal plan 91

INTRODUCTION

The joy that I am feeling right now cannot be explained. This is because you have chosen me and this book as a guide to a new path – the Mediterranean one. The Mediterranean diet is like no other diet in this world and this way of eating is offering many health and weight benefits.

Right after World War II, Ancel Keys, a scientist and his colleague Paul Dudley, later known as President Eisenhower's cardiac physician made a Seven Countries Study together with couple of their colleagues. They included people from United States and people from Crete – Mediterranean island. The study was testing these people of all ages and Keys implemented the Mediterranean diet in this study as well.

The 13,000 men came from Netherlands, United States, Greece, Italy, Yugoslavia and Japan and it was estimated that fruits, vegetables, grains, beans and fish are the healthiest ingredients ever. This applies even after considering the impoverishment of WWII. Interestingly this was also estimated at the start, imagine what else they discovered.

Among everything else it was discovered that Mediterranean way of food consumption can make one person lose and maintain healthy weight. Every chapter included in this book will reveal different story about this diet plan and how can you become able to change your eating patterns. Also, you will find out that Mediterranean diet plan gives extreme amount of energy and you will become motivated

Chapter 1: Why this type of diet is the right for you?

Simply because it contains healthy plant foods and it is low in animal foods. Unlike other diets, Mediterranean diet offers more seafood and fish. Seafood and fish are way better than any other meat and the benefits of them is visible after a week or two of constant consumption. Plus, Mediterranean recipes do not leave you hungry, you are full after eating for a longer period.

With constant exercise and fruits, vegetables, legumes, nuts and whole grains (everything that this diet is) you will become the best version of yourself without doubt. Also, you will learn how to perfectly switch bad ingredients with good ingredients. For example, instead of butter you will start using canola or olive oil. Instead of salt you will start using different herbs and spices. Print out the Mediterranean pyramid of foods and you won't regret it.

These recipes are family friendly and you'll be able to host and enjoy and host many gatherings with your friends as well because they are also friend friendly. Occasional glass of red wine is okay, so you are good to go.

HEALTH BENEFITS

Healthy fats are the key component when it comes to Mediterranean cuisine. Also, let's not forget about the most important thing this diet has – plant-based food. Yes, this diet does not remove many food groups, but the mixture of ingredients won't make you a single problem and you will learn what goes with what in time.

But let's elaborate on the health benefits a little bit more. It is scientifically proven that the Mediterranean diet is able to lower the risk of strokes and heart disease. Every patient that has used this diet style so far, has shown lowered levels of oxidized low-density lipoprotein or LDL cholesterol (the bad cholesterol which gets build up in your arteries and causes problems with your heart.

NO MORE HEART PROBLEMS AND STROKES

One of the main ingredients in the Mediterranean diet, extra virgin olive oil, contains alpha-linolenic acid and the Warwick Medical School delivered a study that indicated how olive oil is able to decrease blood pressure. Not only that but also the olive oil is able to lower hypertension because it keeps human arteries clearer and more dilated. Also, it makes the nitric oxide more bioavailable and you won't have problems with cholesterol levels anymore. Only if of course, you consume olive oil (extra virgin) on regular bases.

If you are feeling numbness, weakness, headaches, confusion, vision problems, dizziness or slurred speech do not worry no more. This diet helps and improves this condition together with the ultimate problem – strokes that are happening due to bleeding in the brain or blocked blood vessel.

IMPROVED VISION

Another thing that would improve after starting with this diet is your vision. This diet will help you prevent or stave off the risk of macular degeneration which happens to adults over 54. This disease brings blindness and occurs to over 10 million Americans. Imagine the benefit in here, imagine being victorious against something that is able to destroy your retina and remove the chance of clear vision. The vegetables this diet promotes, the green leafy ones have lutein and that lowers the chance of experiencing cataracts as well.

WEIGHT LOSS

You probably want to lose weight as well and the search for the perfect diet that will be able to provide you that is endless. Until now. This diet is also able to give you the chance to lose weight naturally and easily with nutrient rich foods. The focus in here is on healthy fats while carbohydrates are not that present. They are still here as pasta or bread of course, but their implementation is generally low. The healthy fats, protein and fiber will allow you to lose weight and at the same time will keep you satisfied. Thanks to these nutrients you won't have cravings for candy, chips or cookies no more. The vegetables that you'll consume will fill your stomach and you won't feel hunger for hours. You won't even experience spike in your blood sugar.

IMPROVED AGILITY

According to studies, 70 percent of the seniors who have risk of developing frailty or other muscle weakness lowered the factors of experiencing that by implementing this diet in their lives.

YOU'LL START ENJOYING NATURAL FOODS

This is probably the best thing that this diet brings because it is kind of a new characteristic that you'll develop. As previously noted, this diet is low in sugar and processed foods so its recipes will bring you closer to organic produced foods thus closer to nature. For example, this diet offers honey instead of sugar and this change is priceless.

IMPROVED ASTHMA SYMPTOMS

Another study which included children revealed that antioxidant diet is able to help them decrease their asthma symptoms and at the same time made them not like eating a food that is quite popular – red meat. Yes, this diet helps children to say no to red meat and yes to plant-based food.

NO MORE ALZHEIMER'S RISK

Those people that choose this diet plant without doubt lower their risk of getting Alzheimer's disease in the future. In fact, the latest study shows that getting Alzheimer's is reduced by 40 percent to those people that consume Mediterranean diet foods. Additional exercises are recommended in the process as well.

HELPS PEOPLE WITH DIABETES

Excessive insulin is controlled with Mediterranean diet. Not every diet is able to do this and not every diet can control blood sugar levels and control your weight at the same time. As I told before this diet is at the same time low in sugar and high in healthy acids. This makes a balance for your body and burns fat while gives you energy at the same time.

The American Heart Association reveals that this diet unlike other diets is low in saturated fat while high in fat. This keeps your hunger under control and delivers amazing weight loss results.

MEDITERRANEAN DIET HELPS YOUR BRAIN

Sugar is usually responsible for the highs and lows when it comes to your mood. This diet does not contain artificial sugar at all this your mood and overall brain health will improve as well.

THE WEIGHT LOSS JOURNEY

Planning breakfast, lunch or dinner is not hard, but the part gets tricky when it comes to snacking time. You should make something for yourself that contains from 150 to 200 calories. For example, you can choose apple, pear, grapefruit and a pinch of salt.

The path that this diet offers is the safest when it comes to losing weight. Everything is healthy here and there won't be bouncing.

But many people ask what happens when the time is stumbling on us and when we do not have time to cook the meals present in here. Well, I and this diet of course have a solution for you. Trust me you will like it.

- Fruit slices – pears and apples
- Nut butter – cashew butter, almond butter and more
- Dates and figs
- Tuna salad
- Crackers
- Greek Yogurt
- Olives
- Pitas
- Hummus

Chapter 2: Your Mindset and this diet

In order to remove the unwanted pounds, you have to set your mindset on it like never before. Do not think about that all the time, start thinking about something entirely else while you are focused on losing weight. Or in other words, keep yourself busy while you consume Mediterranean diet foods and you regularly exercise. Also do not expect quick fixes. Time is all you need and after successfully sticking to the plant you'll start to realize the change and how big it is.

To be sincere, the Mediterranean diet is the one thing that you have been missing for so long. You are already motivated I think so all you have to do is start. You already purchased this book, so you are on the right path.

Write down your reasons for starting this journey and every time you are feeling down, or you lack motivated read them out loud. Write down your goals as well. Start with something small and increase as time passes.

Another important thing that people usually forget are their surroundings. It is important for you to surround with people that are positive. Positive mindset regardless of what you do is important, especially when it comes to losing weight and changing something as diet pattern. This is how you'll become able to develop emotionally, healthy realistic goals (do not forget to set your goals first).

Focus on your sleep and develop a healthy sleeping pattern as well. Recharging and sleeping for more than 7 hours are essential when it comes to weight loss because you need extreme amount of energy and sharpness. Good energy and brain sharpness appear only when one is able to properly relax and recharge in the evening hours.

Chapter 3: Nutrition and Portions

Start being aware of the things you consume now. Develop your management skills and stick to the guidelines that this book gives. What to consume? Well start with:

- Vegetables – raw and leafy
- Fruit
- Legumes
- Grains (one slice of bread is allowed)
- Dairy
- Meat
- Potatoes
- Nuts

This is the food you must start combining and portions that include these ingredients will make you set and ready for reaching your goals.

This is a sustainable diet so you won't have serious problems, but I will be lying if I say that cravings won't appear. If you successfully understand your cravings, you'll remove them and soon be proud of your dietary success. Remember, cravings for certain foods indicate need of something entirely else, something that your body is need of.

So, the adjustments that you have to make regarding the cravings are:

- Remove salty cravings with couple of nuts or seeds because your body want silicon.

- Remove fatty and oily foods with spinach, broccoli, cheese and fish because your body wants calcium and chloride.

- Remove sugary foods with chicken, beef, lamb, liver, cheese, cauliflower and broccoli because your body wants phosphorous and tryptophan.

- Remove chocolate cravings (this is the hardest one) with spinach, nuts, seeds, broccoli and cheese because your body wants magnesium and chromium.

You also have to:

- Learn how to recognize every healthy ingredient on the labels. Take back everything that does not look good to your or that indicates that there are many artificial preservatives present.

- Check your serving size.

- Always calculate your calories intake

- Consume food rich in calcium, iron, fiber, vitamin A and vitamin C.

Do not consume:

- Added sugar or foods like candy, soda, ice cream and more.

- Refined oils – soybean oil, canola oil cottonseed oil and more.

- Trans fats – margarine, soda, processed meats, beverages, table sugar and more.

- Processed meat.

- Refined grains.

Foods that you should consume:

- Seafood and Fish: Mussels, clams, crab, prawns, oysters, shrimp, tuna, mackerel, salmon, trout, sardines, anchovies, and more

- Poultry: Turkey, duck, chicken, and more

- Eggs: Duck, quail, and chicken eggs

- Dairy Products: Contain calcium, B12, and Vitamin A: Greek yogurt, regular yogurt, cheese, plus others

- Tubers: Yams, turnips, potatoes, sweet potatoes, etc.

- Vegetables: Another excellent choice for fiber, and antioxidants: Cucumbers, carrots, Brussels sprouts, tomatoes, onions, broccoli, cauliflower, spinach, kale, eggplant, artichokes, fennel, etc.

- Seedsand Nuts: Provide minerals, vitamins, fiber, and protein: Macadamia nuts, cashews, pumpkin seeds, sunflower seeds, hazelnuts, chestnuts, Brazil nuts, walnuts, almonds, pumpkin seeds, sesame, poppy, and more

- Fruits: Excellent choices for vitamin C, antioxidants, and fiber: Peaches, bananas, apples, figs, dates, pears, oranges, strawberries, melons, grapes, etc.

- Spices and Herbs: Cinnamon, garlic, pepper, nutmeg, rosemary, sage, mint, basil, parsley, etc.

- Whole Grains: Whole grain bread and pasta, buckwheat, whole wheat, barley, corn, whole oats, rye, quinoa, bulgur, couscous 18

- Legumes: Provide vitamins, fiber, carbohydrates, and protein: Chickpeas, pulses, beans, lentils, peanuts, peas

- Healthy Fats: Avocado oil, avocados, olive oil, olive oil products and olives

- Beverages: Water and tea

- White meat: Consume them but remove the visible fat and skin

- Red meat: You can consume lamb, pork, and beef in small amounts

- Potatoes: Prepare them with caution but consume them because they are excellent source of potassium, vitamin b, vitamin c and fibers.

- Desserts and sweets: consume cakes, biscuits and sweets in extra small amounts.

There is one thing that you can implement that will make your journey even more beautiful – spices and herbs! Traditional Mediterranean diet is filled with different spices and herbs and each has a different health benefit! Believe it or not herbs and spices are able to do that and that is one of the main reasons why people implement them in their diet. Here are the spices you must include and the benefits they bring:

- Anise – improves digestion, reduces nausea and alleviates cramps.
- Bay leaf – treats migraines.
- Basil – aids digestion and reduces anxiety and stress.
- Black pepper – promotes nutrient absorption and speeds up your metabolism.
- Cayenne pepper – increases metabolism and controls your appetite.
- Sweet and spicy cloves – relive pain, gum and tooth pain. Also, kill bacteria, fungal infections and aid digestive problems.
- Fennel – improves bone health.
- Garlic – improves blood sugar levels and helps you lose weight.
- Ginger – serves as diuretic and increases urine elimination.
- Marjoram – promotes healthy digestion and fights type 2 diabetes.
- Mint – treats nasal congestion, nausea, dizziness and headaches.
- Oregano – treats common cold and reduces infections. It also relieves menstrual pain.
- Parsley – improves your skin, prostate, dental health and blood circulation.
- Rosemary – increases hair growth, reduces stress, inflammation and improves pain.
- Sage – improves your digestion problems.
- Thyme – has antibacterial properties.

Chapter 4: Exercise

Mediterranean diet is extremely flexible, and you won't have problems while being out with friends. Many recipes in the restaurants come from this particular diet so, you are good to go as long as you do not eat junk food and food that is high in sugar.

Eat slowly and chew your food better. Put your utensils down between bites because that is going to help you slow down the process of eating.

The tips above will help you a lot, but nothing will help you more in this journey than exercising. Two years ago, one scientific research that mainly focused on the Mediterranean diet revealed that this diet is extremely beneficial and gets its full potential when exercise is included. So, to keep your weight under control and to lose weight at the same time you must exercise.

Do not force yourself, start with something easy and small. Spend 30 to 60 minutes daily on that part. Walk, run, do yoga, swim, ride a bike, or simply infiltrate yourself into a regular exercise program online or in a gym near you.

Regular physical activity does not improve only your look, it also improves your strength, mood and balance.

Chapter 5: The recipes in this book

This book contains 500 recipes in total. Each recipe is designed according to the rules Mediterranean diet has. Every recipe is healthy, and every recipe should be made with the best ingredients available – the organic ones. There is also a section for vegans and vegetarians. We wanted to include every person possible in this journey because this journey is all about health and improving yourself and the way you eat. At the bottom of this book you will find a meal plan that we think is going to help you a lot in the few first months. The start won't be that hard, but it is going to be challenging I must admit.

The cooking skills

It is important to know that the Mediterranean do not require hours and hours in the kitchen. The way these recipes are prepared is easy and convenient.

Breakfast Recipes

Seafood Omelet

COOKING: 20 MIN   SERVES: 2

INGREDIENTS

Filling:
1/4 cup chicken broth
1 tablespoon Dijon mustard
1/4 cup heavy cream
tablespoons butter
1 (6 ounce) can crab
1 (6 ounce) can salad shrimp
Sauce:
1/4 cup heavy cream
1 teaspoon Dijon mustard
1 cup shredded Cheddar cheese
1 dash nutmeg
Salt and pepper to taste
Omelets:
4 eggs, beaten
1/4 cup heavy cream Salt and pepper to taste

Nutritional Value: 312 calories per serving

DIRECTIONS

1. Prepare the filling by stirring Dijon mustard into chicken broth in a saucepan until dissolved. Bring to a simmer over medium-high heat, then add 1/4 cup cream and 2 tablespoons butter. Reduce heat to medium, and simmer until reduced by half, then stir in crab and shrimp; keep warm over low heat.
2. Prepare the sauce by warming 1/4 cup cream, and 1 teaspoon mustard over medium heat. Once hot, whisk in the shredded cheese, then season to taste with nutmeg, salt, and pepper. Keep warm over low heat.
3. Whisk eggs, 1/4 cup cream, salt, and pepper together until smooth. Heat an 8-inch non-stick skillet over medium heat, and lightly oil with cooking spray. Pour 1/4 cup of the egg mixture into hot pan, and swirl to make a thin, even layer of egg. Cook until firmed, then flip and cook for a few seconds more to firm the other side.
4. To prepare omelets, spoon some of the seafood filling into the lower half of each omelet. Roll up into a cylinder. Serve 2 per person bathed with Cheddar sauce.

Breakfast Recipes

Eggs with Sausages and Spinach

COOKING: 20 MIN

SERVES: 2

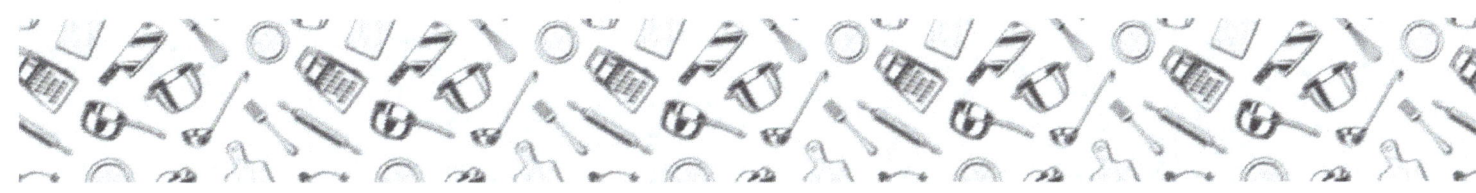

INGREDIENTS

1-pound bulk hot Italian sausage
2 large onions, finely chopped
1/2-pound sliced fresh mushrooms
2 garlic cloves, minced
1/4 teaspoon salt
1/4 teaspoon ground nutmeg
1/4 teaspoon dried oregano
1/4 teaspoon pepper
2 tablespoons olive oil
8 cups torn fresh spinach 8 eggs
1/4 teaspoon hot pepper sauce
1 cup shredded Monterey Jack cheese

Nutritional Value: 471 calories per serving

DIRECTIONS

1. Crumble sausage into a 10-in. ovenproof skillet; cook over medium heat until no longer pink. Drain and set aside. In the same skillet, saute the onions, mushrooms, garlic and seasonings in oil until vegetables are tender. Add spinach in batches; cook over medium- low heat for 3-4 minutes or until spinach begins to wilt.
2. In a large bowl, whisk eggs and hot pepper sauce. Return sausage to skillet; add egg mixture. As eggs set, lift edges, letting uncooked portion flow underneath. Cook until eggs are nearly set, about 8-10 minutes.
3. Meanwhile, preheat broiler. Broil egg mixture 6 in. from the heat for 30-60 seconds or until set. Sprinkle with cheese; broil 30 seconds longer or until melted. Cut into wedges. Serve immediately.

Breakfast Recipes

Terrine for Breakfast

COOKING: 20 MIN   SERVES: 2

INGREDIENTS

1 lb. sweet Italian sausage, casings removed
1 lb. chicken livers
1 medium onion, chopped
1/4 cup flour
1/4 cup brandy
1 tsp. salt
1/4 tsp. allspice
1/4 tsp. nutmeg
pinch ground cloves
1/4 tsp. pepper
2 garlic cloves chopped
3 eggs
1/2 lb. sliced bacon

Nutritional Value: 312 calories per serving

DIRECTIONS

1. In a large skillet cook sausage, stirring until brown. Drain on paper towels, set aside in bowl.
2. In blender combine remaining Ingredients except bacon, for 45 seconds. Stir in sausage.
3. Preheat oven to 350 degrees. Line loaf pan with heavy foil, letting 3" hang over the sides. Place bacon slices crosswise across bottom and up sides, letting slices overhang pan. Pour in sausage mixture, fold bacon over top. Place loaf pan in shallow pan; pour 1" hot water into shallow pan. Bake 1-1/2 hours.
4. Remove loaf pan from water, fold foil over top. Place heavy canon terrine to weight down. Press firmly 2 minutes. Refrigerate with weight until firm, about 6 hours.
5. To remove terrine, loosen foil from sides of pan, grasp ends of foil, and lift out. Cut into slices.

Breakfast Recipes

Frittata with Asparagus and Onions

COOKING: 20 MIN   SERVES: 2

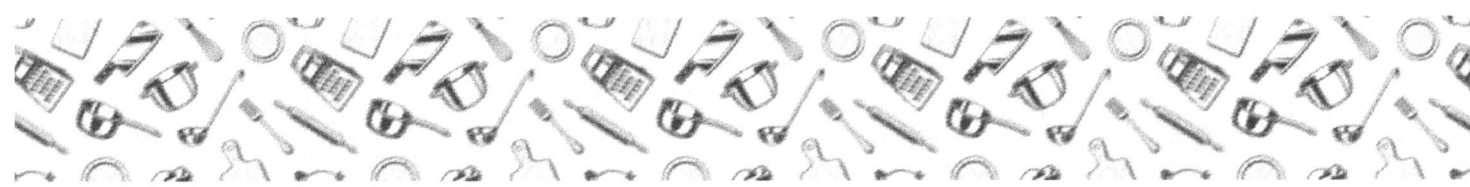

INGREDIENTS

2 tablespoons olive oil
2 potatoes, shredded
1/4 cup chopped onion
1/2 teaspoon salt
1/4 teaspoon fresh ground black pepper
1-pound asparagus, trimmed and cut into 2-inch pieces
1 cup diced ham
6 eggs
1 tablespoon milk
1/2 cup shredded mozzarella cheese
1/2 cup shredded white Cheddar cheese
1 tablespoon chopped fresh basil

Nutritional Value: 372 calories per serving

DIRECTIONS

1. Preheat an oven to 350 degrees F (175 degrees C). Grease a 9x13 inch baking dish.
2. Heat the olive oil in a large skillet over medium heat; cook and stir the shredded potato and onion in the hot oil until the potatoes begin to brown, about 5 minutes. Season with salt and pepper. Add the asparagus and ham and continue cooking until the asparagus is tender, another 5 to 7 minutes, transfer to the prepared baking dish. Whisk the eggs and milk together in a small bowl; pour evenly over the dish. Scatter the mozzarella and white Cheddar cheeses over the top of the potato mixture.
3. Bake in the preheated oven until set in the middle, 20 to 25 minutes. Garnish with the basil to serve.

Breakfast Recipes

Italian Cheese Toast

COOKING: 20 MIN

SERVES: 2

INGREDIENTS

1-1/4 cups half and half
1 tbsp. olive or salad oil
1 tsp. cornstarch
1/2 tsp. paprika
1 tbsp. capers
1 12" loaf Italian bread
1 8 oz. package Mozzarella cheese
1 tbsp. chopped parsley

Nutritional Value: 302 calories per serving

1.

DIRECTIONS

1. In 2-qt. saucepan, combine first 4 Ingredients. Cook over medium
2. heat, until boiling, stirring constantly. Boil 1 minute. Reduce heat, stir in capers, cover, keep warm.
3. Preheat broiler. From Italian bread, diagonally cut 8 one-inch thick slices (save remaining bread).
4. Toast bread in broiler on each side. Put sliced cheese on each piece and broil until melted.
5. Spoon cream mixture over cheese. Garnish with parsley. Serve immediately.

Breakfast Recipes

 **Omelet with Spinach, Ham and Cheese**

COOKING: 20 MIN   SERVES: 2

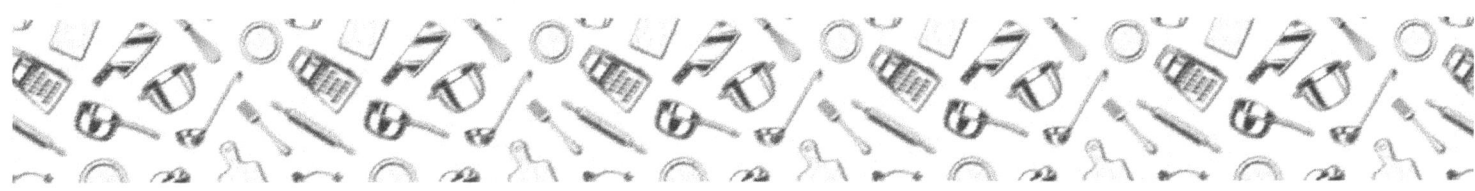

INGREDIENTS

2 eggs
2 tablespoons water
1 teaspoon butter Salt and pepper
1/4 cup shredded Italian cheese blend
1/4 cup baby spinach
1/4 cup finely chopped ham

Nutritional Value: 471 calories per serving

DIRECTIONS

1. Beat eggs and water in small bowl until blended.
2. Heat butter in 7 to 10-inch nonstick omelet pan or skillet over medium-high heat until hot. Tilt pan to coat bottom. Pour in egg mixture. Mixture should set immediately at edges.
3. Gently push cooked portions from edges toward the center with inverted turner so that uncooked eggs can reach the hot pan surface. Continue cooking, tilting pan and gently moving cooked portions as needed.
4. When top surface of eggs is thickened and no visible liquid egg remains, season with salt and pepper. Place cheese on one side of omelet; top with spinach and ham. Fold omelet in half with turner. With a quick flip of the wrist, turn pan and invert or slide omelet onto plate. Serve immediately.

Breakfast Recipes

Orange Pancakes

COOKING: 20 MIN

SERVES: 2

INGREDIENTS

7 tablespoons sugar, divided
1 1/2 teaspoons cornstarch
1 1/2 cups orange juice, divided
2 cups biscuit/baking mix
2 eggs
3/4 cup milk

Nutritional Value: 200 calories per serving

DIRECTIONS

1. In a saucepan, mix 4 tablespoons sugar, cornstarch and 3/4 cup orange juice; stir until smooth. Bring to a boil; cook and stir for 2 minutes. Remove from heat; cool to lukewarm.
2. Meanwhile, Mix biscuit mix and remaining sugar in a bowl. Beat the eggs, milk and remaining orange juice; stir into dry Ingredients just until moistened. Pour the batter by 1/4 cupfuls onto a lightly greased hot griddle; turn when bubbles form on top of pancakes. Cook until second side is golden brown. Serve with the orange sauce..

Breakfast Recipes

Oatmeal Apricot Bites

COOKING: 20 MIN   SERVES: 2

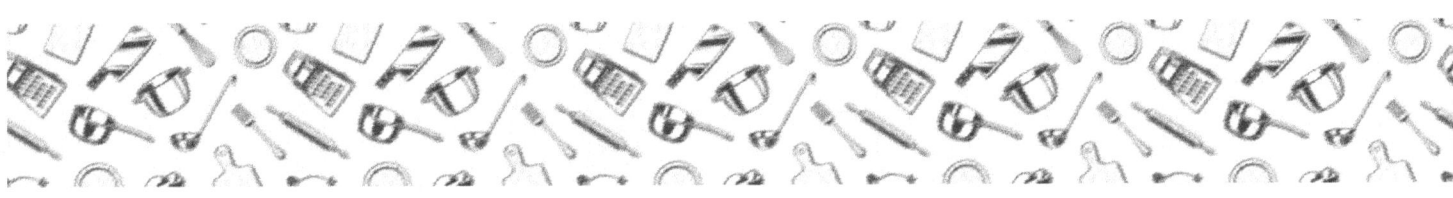

INGREDIENTS

3/4 cup unsweetened applesauce
1/3 cup packed brown sugar
1/3 cup honey
1/2 cup whole wheat flour
1/2 cup all-purpose flour
1/2 teaspoon baking soda
1/2 teaspoon baking powder
1/4 teaspoon salt
1/2 teaspoon ground cinnamon
1/4 teaspoon ground nutmeg
1/2 cup rolled oats
1 teaspoon vanilla extract
1 teaspoon almond extract
1/2 cup chopped dried apricots
1/4 cup sliced almonds
1/4 cup dried cranberries

Nutritional Value: 200 calories per serving

DIRECTIONS

1. Preheat oven to 350 degrees F (175 degrees C). Lightly grease a baking sheet.
2. In a large bowl, blend the applesauce, brown sugar, and honey. In a separate bowl, sift together the whole wheat flour, all-purpose flour, baking soda, baking powder, salt, cinnamon, and nutmeg. Blend the flour mixture into the applesauce mixture. Fold in the oats, vanilla extract, almond extract, apricots, almonds, and cranberries. Drop the batter by rounded teaspoonfuls onto the prepared baking sheet.
3. Bake 12 to 15 minutes in the preheated oven, until golden brown. Cool on wire racks.

Breakfast Recipes

Olive oil and Onion Bread for Breakfast

COOKING: 20 MIN　　　　　　　　　　　　　　　　　　　　SERVES: 2

INGREDIENTS

2 (.25 ounce) packages rapid rise yeast
1/2 cup warm water
2 tablespoons extra-virgin olive oil
2 large red onions, diced
7 cups bread flour
1 1/2 teaspoons salt
1/2 teaspoon white raw honey
1/4 cup chopped fresh dill
1/4 teaspoon garlic powder (optional)
2 cups pitted kalamata olives, chopped
1 3/4 cups warm water

Nutritional Value: 126 calories per serving

DIRECTIONS

1. Sprinkle the yeast over 1/2 cup of warm water in a small bowl. The water should be no more than 100 degrees F (40 degrees C). Let stand for 5 minutes until the yeast softens and begins to form a creamy foam.
2. Heat a large skillet over medium heat and add the olive oil and the onions. Cook and stir for 3 minutes, or until onions are soft.
3. Remove the onions from heat and reserve
4. Mix the bread flour, salt, raw honey, dill, garlic powder, olives, and cooked onions in a large bowl and mix well. Add the yeast mixture and the remaining 1 3/4 cup water. Mix well until the Ingredients have pulled together and have formed a sticky dough. Turn the dough out onto a lightly floured surface and knead until smooth and elastic, about 8 minutes.
5. Lightly oil a large bowl, then place the dough in the bowl and turn to coat with oil. Cover with a light cloth and let rise in a warm place (80 to 95 degrees F (27 to 35 degrees C)) until doubled in volume, about 1 hour.
6. Lightly grease two baking sheets. Deflate the risen dough and turn it out onto a lightly floured surface. Use a knife to divide the dough into two equal pieces-don't tear it. Shape into dough into round loaves and place the loaves into the prepared pans. Cover the loaves with a damp cloth and let rise until doubled in volume, about 40 minutes.
7. Preheat an oven to 450 degrees F (230 degrees C).
8. Bake loaves in the preheated oven until the tops are golden brown and the bottoms sound hollow when tapped, about 40 minutes.
9. Cool slightly before slicing..

Breakfast Recipes

Scrambled Eggs

COOKING: 20 MIN

SERVES: 2

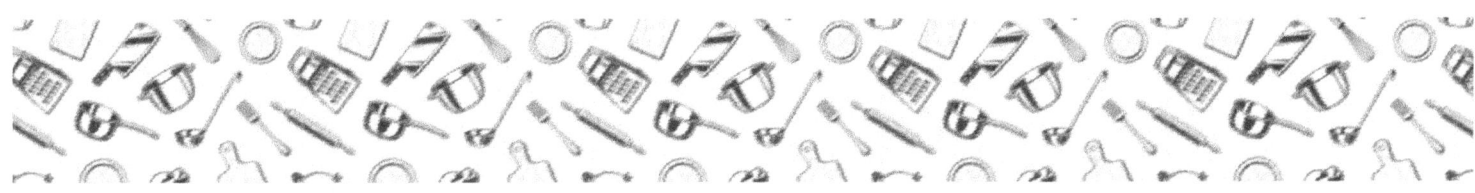

INGREDIENTS

Nutritional Value: 200 calories per serving

DIRECTIONS

1. Put two tablespoonfuls of butter in a shallow frying pan. Add a tablespoonful of water to each egg. Six eggs are quite enough for four people. Add a half teaspoonful of salt, and a saltspoonful of pepper.
2. Give two or three beats--enough to break the eggs; turn them into the frying pan, on the hot butter. Constantly scrape from the bottom of the pan with a fork, while they are cooking. Serve with a garnish of broiled bacon and toast.

Breakfast Recipes

Sandwiches with Almond Butter

COOKING: 20 MIN   SERVES: 2

INGREDIENTS

2 tablespoons almond butter
1 tablespoon strawberry jam
1/2 bananas, sliced
2 fresh strawberries, sliced
2 slices whole-grain bread

Nutritional Value: 454 calories per serving

DIRECTIONS

3. Spread almond butter over one side of one slice of bread. Arrange strawberries and bananas over almond butter. Spread jam over one side of remaining slice of bread. Place over fruit to make a sandwich..

Breakfast Recipes

 **Western Frittata**

COOKING: 20 MIN SERVES: 2

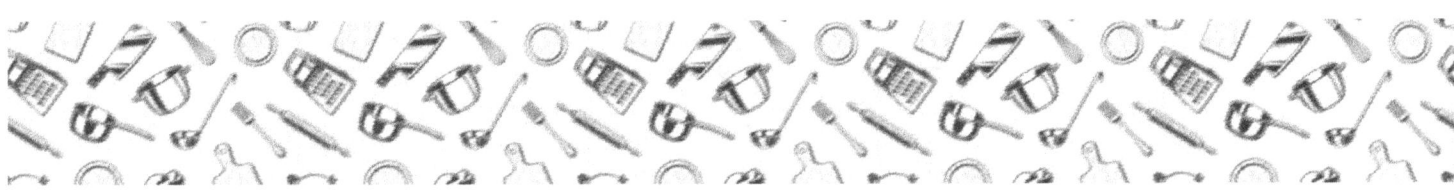

INGREDIENTS

2 tbsp. butter
4 oz. Canadian bacon
2 medium onions
7 eggs
1/2 cup Swiss cheese
1/4 tsp. pepper

Nutritional Value: 147 calories per serving

DIRECTIONS

4. In 10" skillet heat 2 tbsp. butter over medium heat. Add bacon sliced and cut into 1/2" strips, cook 1 minute. Add sliced onions, cook 3 minutes, stirring frequently; remove from heat.
5. In bowl beat eggs, grated cheese, pepper and bacon-onion mixture. In skillet melt butter over medium heat. Add egg mixture, reduce heat to medium-low, cook 10-15 minutes until bottom is set. Meanwhile, preheat broiler. Broil frittata until top is set and lightly browned, about 3 minutes..

Breakfast Recipes

Scrambled Eggs from Greece

COOKING: 20 MIN   SERVES: 2

INGREDIENTS

1 tablespoon butter
3 eggs
1 teaspoon water
1/2 cup crumbled feta cheese salt and pepper to taste

Nutritional Value: 244 calories per serving

DIRECTIONS

6. Heat butter in a skillet over medium-high heat. Beat eggs and water together, then pour into pan. Add feta cheese, and cook, stirring occasionally to scramble. Season with salt and pepper.

Breakfast Recipes

Avocados Stuffed

COOKING: 20 MIN

SERVES: 2

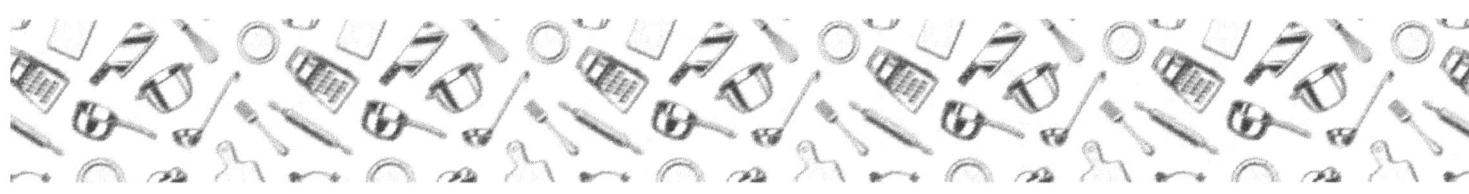

INGREDIENTS

1/2 cup flaked cooked crabmeat
1/2 cup cooked small shrimp
2 tablespoons peeled and diced cucumber
1 tablespoon mayonnaise
1 teaspoon chopped fresh parsley
1 pinch salt
1 pinch ground black pepper
1 pinch paprika
1 avocado

Nutritional Value: 400 calories per serving

DIRECTIONS

7. In a bowl, mix the crab, shrimp, cucumber, mayonnaise, and parsley. Season with salt, and pepper. Cover, and chill until serving.
8. Slice the avocados lengthwise and remove the pit. Scoop out the flesh of the avocado, leaving about 1/2 inch on the peel. Spoon the seafood mixture into the hollowed centers of the avocado halves. Sprinkle the tops with paprika.

Breakfast Recipes

Spinach Pancakes

COOKING: 20 MIN   SERVES: 2

INGREDIENTS

4 tablespoons all-purpose flour
2 eggs
1 (10 ounce) package frozen spinach, thawed and drained salt and pepper to taste
1/2 teaspoon paprika
2 tablespoons olive oil

Nutritional Value: 200 calories per serving

DIRECTIONS

9. In a medium bowl, mix together flour and eggs. Stir in spinach, and season with salt and pepper to taste and paprika.
10. Heat olive oil in a large skillet. Drop spinach mixture into the oil by the spoonful and flatten into patties. Cook until browned on both sides. Remove to paper towels to drain. Serve warm.

Breakfast Recipes

French Toast with Pecans

COOKING: 20 MIN   SERVES: 2

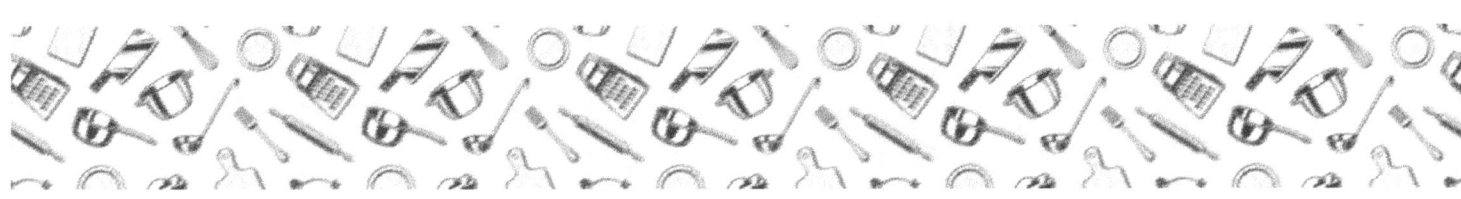

INGREDIENTS

4 eggs
2/3 cup orange juice
1/3 cup milk
1/4 cup white sugar
1/4 teaspoon nutmeg
1/4 teaspoon vanilla extract
1/2 (1 pound) loaf Italian bread, cut into 1-inch slices
1/3 cup butter, melted
1/2 cup chopped pecans
2 tablespoons grated orange zest

Nutritional Value: 500 calories per serving

DIRECTIONS

11. In a large bowl, beat together eggs, orange juice, milk, sugar, nutmeg and vanilla extract. Place bread slices in a tightly spaced single layer in the bottom of a flat dish or baking pan. Pour milk mixture over bread, cover and refrigerate overnight, turning once.
12. When ready to cook, preheat oven to 350 degrees F (175 degrees C).
13. Coat a jelly roll pan, or rimmed baking sheet, evenly with the melted butter. Arrange soaked bread slices in a single layer on pan.
14. Sprinkle evenly with orange peel and pecans.
15. Bake in preheated oven until golden, 20 to 25 minutes. Check slices during last 10 minutes of baking time to avoid burning.

Breakfast Recipes

Oven Omelet with Pears

COOKING: 20 MIN

SERVES: 2

INGREDIENTS

2 tablespoons butter or margarine
1/4 teaspoon ground cinnamon
1/8 teaspoon ground ginger
3 tablespoons sugar, divided
3 medium pears, peeled and thinly sliced
2 tablespoons all-purpose flour
4 eggs, separated
1/2 teaspoon vanilla extract

Nutritional Value: 312 calories per serving

DIRECTIONS

16. In an ovenproof 10-in. skillet, melt butter over medium heat. Stir in cinnamon, ginger and 1 tablespoon of sugar. cook for 1 minute or until the sugar is dissolved. Reduce heat; add the pears. Cook for 5 minutes or until softened, stirring occasionally. remove from the heat; arrange the pears evenly in the skillet.
17. In a bowl, whisk the flour, 1 tablespoon sugar, egg yolks and vanilla until smooth. In a small mixing bowl, beat the egg whites with remaining sugar until stiff peaks form. Gently fold into the egg yolk mixture just until blended. Spread over the pears. Bake, uncovered, at 400 degrees F for 10 minutes or until puffed and golden brown.

Breakfast Recipes

Omelet with Baby Spinach

COOKING: 20 MIN

SERVES: 2

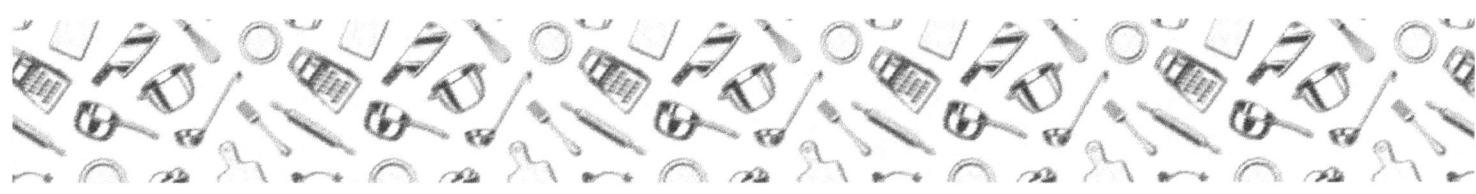

INGREDIENTS

2 eggs
1 cup torn baby spinach leaves
1 1/2 tablespoons grated Parmesan cheese
1/4 teaspoon onion powder
1/8 teaspoon ground nutmeg salt and pepper to taste

Nutritional Value: 258 calories per serving

DIRECTIONS

18. In a bowl, beat the eggs, and stir in the baby spinach and Parmesan cheese. Season with onion powder, nutmeg, salt, and pepper.
19. In a small skillet coated with cooking spray over medium heat, cook the egg mixture about 3 minutes, until partially set. Flip with a spatula and continue cooking 2 to 3 minutes. Reduce heat to low, and continue cooking 2 to 3 minutes, or to desired doneness.

Breakfast Recipes

 Vegetable Poached Eggs

COOKING: 20 MIN   SERVES: 2

INGREDIENTS

1 1/2 tablespoons olive oil
1 cup fresh asparagus, trimmed and coarsely chopped
1 cup carrots, julienned
1/4 cup spaghetti sauce
4 eggs
salt and pepper to taste

Nutritional Value: 236 calories per serving

DIRECTIONS

20. In a large frying pan, heat the oil over medium high heat. Add the asparagus, carrots and spaghetti sauce; cook on medium high heat until vegetables are soft. You may add a little water if necessary.
21. Push the vegetables to the side of the pan to create four spaces for the eggs. Crack eggs directly into the holes, being careful not to break the yolk. Cook until eggs are done, but the yolk is still soft.
22. Season with salt and pepper to taste. Remove from heat and serve immediately.

Breakfast Recipes

Italian Sandwich for Breakfast

COOKING: 20 MIN

SERVES: 2

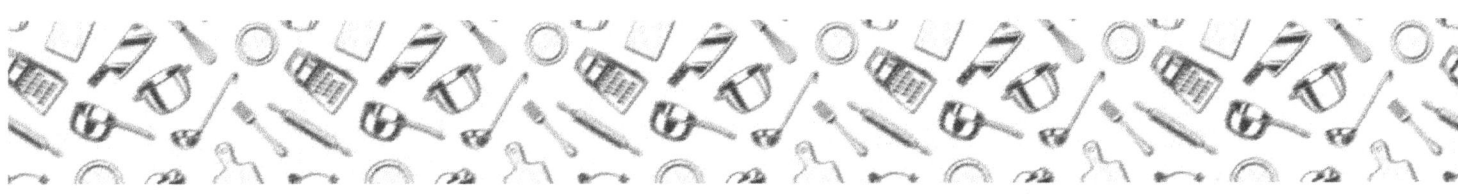

INGREDIENTS

12 sweet Italian sausages
1/4 cup water
2 medium onions
2 tbsp. olive/salad oil
4 5" long hard rolls
5 green or red peppers

Nutritional Value: 369 calories per serving

DIRECTIONS

1. In skillet, place sausages, add water. Cover, simmer 5 minutes.
2. Remove cover and cook 15 minutes or until browned, turning occasionally.
3. Cut onions into thin slices, peppers into 1/2" strips. In hot oil saute onions until limp. Add peppers and cook over medium
4. heat until peppers are tender, about 10 minutes. Add cooked sausage.
5. Split rolls in half lengthwise. Layer bottom of each roll with
6. onions and pepper and 3 sausages. Spread top of roll with mayo, butter or ketchup.

Breakfast Recipes

Scalloped Eggs

COOKING: 20 MIN

SERVES: 2

INGREDIENTS

4 hard-boiled eggs
2 tablespoonfuls of butter
2 level tablespoonfuls of flour
1/2 pint of milk
1 cupful of finely chopped cold cooked chicken or fish
1 teaspoonful of salt
1 saltspoonful of pepper

Nutritional Value: 147 calories per serving

DIRECTIONS

1. Chop the eggs rather fine. Rub the butter and flour together, add the milk, stir until boiling, add the salt and pepper. Put a layer of eggs in the bottom of a casserole, or baking dish, then a layer of the fish or chicken, then a little white sauce, and so continue until the
2. Ingredients are used. Dust the top thickly with breadcrumbs and bake in a moderate oven until nicely browned.

Breakfast Recipes

Avocado and Egg Sandwich

COOKING: 20 MIN

SERVES: 2

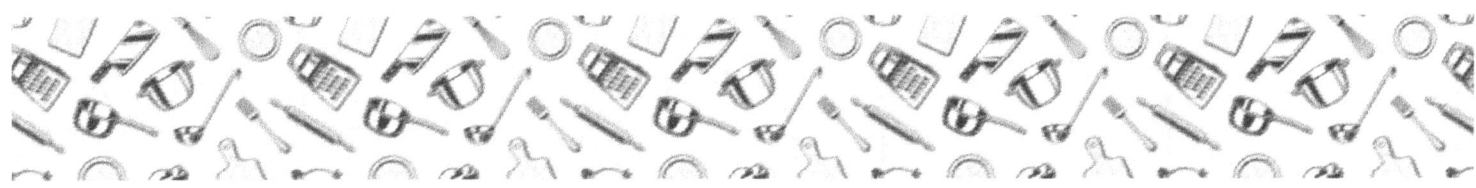

INGREDIENTS

4 bread slices
1 avocado
10 asparagus spears
1 hardboiled egg
Olive oil
Pepper

Nutritional Value: 309 calories per serving

DIRECTIONS

1. Peel and mash the avocado. Toast the bread.
2. Prepare the sandwich by using the mustard with a layer of the avocado.
3. Add the asparagus spears and eggs.
4. Give it a drizzle of oil along with some salt and pepper. Close and serve.

Breakfast Recipes

Potato Pancakes

COOKING: 20 MIN SERVES: 2

INGREDIENTS

5 potatoes, peeled and shredded
2 eggs, beaten
1 onion, finely chopped
3 tablespoons all-purpose flour salt and pepper to taste
3 tablespoons olive oil

Nutritional Value: 412 calories per serving

DIRECTIONS

1. In a large bowl, stir together potatoes, eggs, onion, flour, salt and pepper.
2. In a large skillet, heat oil over medium high heat. Drop large spoonfuls of the potato batter into the skillet and flatten cakes slightly with a spatula. Cook for about 4 minutes on each side, until golden brown. Serve immediately..

Breakfast Recipes

Tuna Melt Sandwich

COOKING: 20 MIN

SERVES: 2

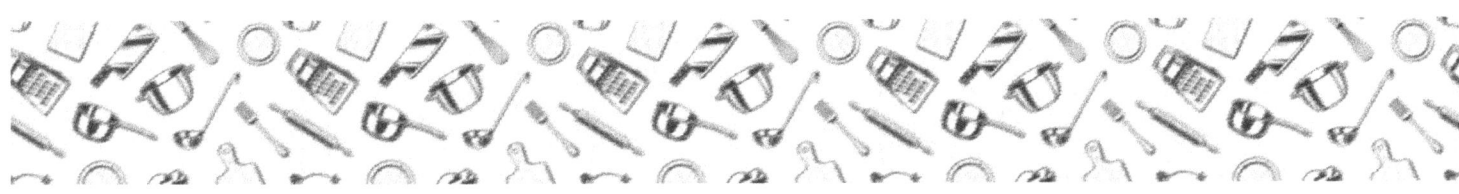

INGREDIENTS

3/4 cup chopped celery
3/4 cup diced Cheddar cheese
1 (6 ounce) can tuna, drained and flaked
1 small onion, chopped
1/4 cup mayonnaise
1/8 teaspoon salt
1/4 cup butter or olive oil, softened
6 hamburger buns, split

Nutritional Value: 258 calories per serving

DIRECTIONS

1. In a bowl, Mix the first six Ingredients; set aside. Spread butter over slice sides of buns. Spread tuna mixture on bun bottoms; replace tops. Wrap in foil. Bake at 350 degrees F for 15 minutes or until the cheese is melted.

Breakfast Recipes

Omelet from Apples

COOKING: 20 MIN   SERVES: 2

INGREDIENTS

9 Large tart apples
4 Eggs
1 cup of sugar
1 tablespoonful of button
Cinnamon or other spices as necessary

Nutritional Value: 458 calories per serving

DIRECTIONS

1. Stew the apples till they are very soft; mash them so that there will be no lumps; add the butter, sugar and spices while they are still warm; but let them cool before putting in the beaten eggs; bake this till it is brown; you may put it all in a shallow pudding-dish or in two tin plates to bake.

Breakfast Recipes

Curried Tuna Melt

COOKING: 20 MIN

SERVES: 2

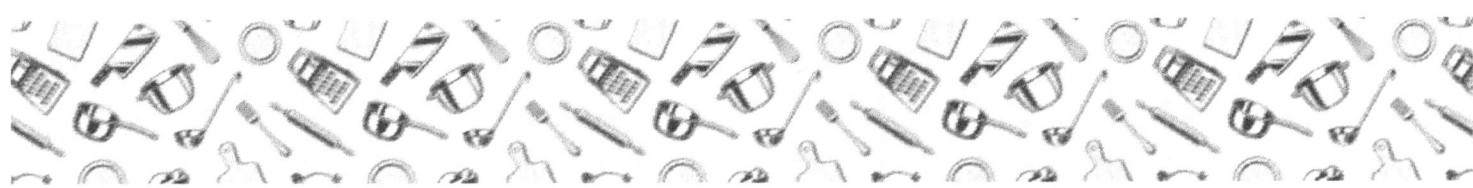

INGREDIENTS

(6 ounce) can tuna, drained and flaked
1/4 cup thinly sliced celery
1/4 cup mayonnaise
2 tablespoons thinly sliced green onions
2 tablespoons raisins
2 teaspoons lemon juice
1/4 teaspoon salt
1/4 teaspoon curry powder
2 English muffins, split and toasted
4 slices Cheddar cheese

Nutritional Value: 444 calories per serving

DIRECTIONS

1. In a small bowl, Mix tuna, celery, mayonnaise, onions, raisins, lemon juice, salt and curry powder. Spread about 1/4 cup on each muffin half: top with cheese. Broil 4 in. from the heat for 1-2 minutes or until cheese is melted.

Breakfast Recipes

Scrambled Eggs with Shrimps

COOKING: 20 MIN

SERVES: 2

INGREDIENTS

6 eggs
1 can of shrimps or its equivalent in fresh shrimps
1 green pepper
1/2 pint of strained tomato
1/2 teaspoonful of salt

Nutritional Value: 147 calories per serving

DIRECTIONS

1. Beat the eggs until well mixed, without separating. Put the butter in a saucepan, add the pepper, chopped; shake until the pepper is soft, add the tomato and all the seasoning, and the shrimps. Bring to boiling point, push to the back of the stove where it will simmer while you scramble the eggs. Put the scrambled eggs on toast in the center of a platter pour over and around the shrimp mixture and send to the table..

Lunch Recipes

Chicken with Almonds and Oranges

COOKING: 20 MIN   SERVES: 2

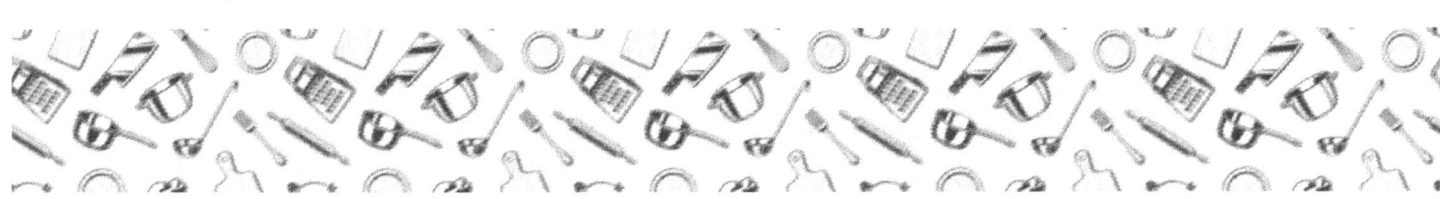

INGREDIENTS

10 tablespoons all-purpose flour, divided
2 eggs
3/4 cup ground almonds
6 (4 ounce) skinless, boneless chicken breast halves
4 tablespoons butter or olive oil, divided
1/3 cup chopped onion
1/4 teaspoon poultry seasoning
1 1/2 cups milk
1/3 cup orange marmalade
1/4 cup orange juice
1/2 teaspoon grated orange peel
1 teaspoon salt
1/4 teaspoon pepper Hot cooked rice

Nutritional Value: 478 calories per serving

DIRECTIONS

1. Place 1/2 cup flour in a shallow bowl. In another bowl, lightly beat the eggs. Place the almonds in a third bowl. Coat chicken with flour, then dip in eggs and roll in almonds. In a skillet over medium-high heat, cook the chicken in 2 tablespoons butter on both sides until juices run clear, about 10 minutes. Remove and keep warm. In the same skillet, saute the onion in remaining butter until tender. Stir in poultry seasoning and remaining flour until blended. Gradually stir in milk until smooth. Bring to a boil; cook and stir for 2 minutes.
2. Remove from the heat; stir in the orange marmalade, orange juice and peel, salt and pepper. Pour over the chicken. Serve with rice if desired.

Lunch Recipes

Halibut with Salsa

COOKING: 20 MIN   SERVES: 2

INGREDIENTS

1/3 cup
orange juice
2 tablespoons canola oil
2 tablespoons lime juice
1 tablespoon brown sugar
2 teaspoons grated lime peel
1 garlic clove, minced
1/2 teaspoon salt
4 (6 ounce) halibut steaks
Salsa:
2 cups chopped fresh or frozen peaches
1/4 cup chopped sweet red pepper
1/4 cup chopped red onion
1 jalapeno pepper, seeded and chopped*
2 tablespoons orange juice
1 tablespoon minced fresh cilantro
2 teaspoons lime juice
1/4 teaspoon salt

DIRECTIONS

1. In a bowl, combine the first seven Ingredients; mix well. Remove 1/4 cup for basting; cover and refrigerate. Pour remaining marinade into a large resealable plastic bag; add the halibut. Seal bag and turn to coat; refrigerate for 2 hours. In a bowl, combine salsa Ingredients; cover and refrigerate until serving.
2. If grilling the fish, coat grill rack with nonstick cooking spray before starting the grill. Drain and discard marinade from fish. Grill, uncovered, over medium heat or broil 4-6 in. from the heat for 4-6 minutes on each side or until fish flakes easily with a fork, basting occasionally with reserved marinade. Serve with peach salsa..

Nutritional Value: 446 calories per serving

Lunch Recipes

Tomato Spinach and Bean Burrito

COOKING: 20 MIN

SERVES: 2

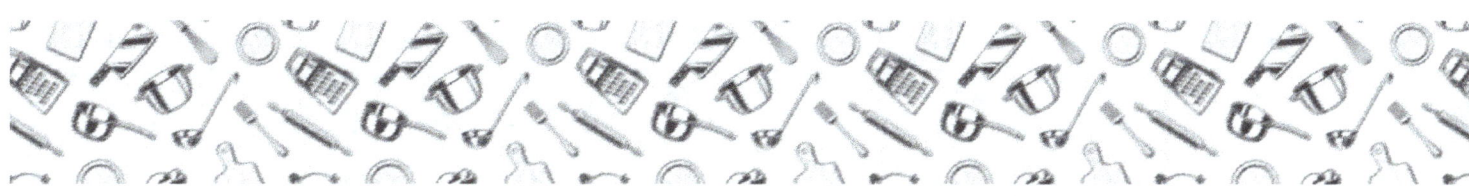

INGREDIENTS

2 tablespoons olive oil
1 cup diced onion
3 cloves garlic, minced
2 tablespoons chili powder, or to taste
1 teaspoon ground cumin
1/4 cup water
4 cups chopped fresh tomatoes
1 (15 ounce) can kidney beans, drained and rinsed
salt to taste
1 (10 ounce) package frozen chopped spinach, thawed and drained
4 (10 inch) flour tortillas
1 ripe avocado, sliced
4 tablespoons sour cream
4 tablespoons salsa

Nutritional Value:

580 calories per serving

DIRECTIONS

1. Heat oil in a large skillet on medium-high heat. Sauté onion and garlic for 5 minutes. Stir in chili powder and cumin and cook 1 minute. Stir in water, tomato, kidney beans and salt. Bring to a boil, then reduce heat and simmer for 20 minutes.
2. Stir in spinach and cook 5 minutes more. Spoon 1/4 of the bean mixture into the middle of a warm tortilla. Wrap and garnish with avocado, sour cream and salsa..

Lunch Recipes

Steak Stuffed with Spinach

COOKING: 20 MIN   SERVES: 2

INGREDIENTS

1 (10 ounce) package frozen chopped spinach, thawed and drained
1 (7 ounce) jar roasted red peppers, drained
1 egg white
1/2 cup seasoned breadcrumbs
1/4 cup grated Parmesan cheese
1/4 cup sunflower kernels, toasted
1 garlic clove, minced
1/2 teaspoon salt
1 (1 1/2-pound) flank steak

Nutritional Value: 356 calories per serving

DIRECTIONS

1. In a bowl, combine the first eight Ingredients; mix well.
2. Cut steak horizontally from a long edge to within 1/2 in. of opposite edge; open (like a book) and flatten to 1/2-in. thickness. Spread spinach mixture over the steak to within 1 in. of edges. Roll up, jelly-roll style, starting with a long side, tie with kitchen string. Place in a greased 13-in. x 9-in. x 2-in. baking dish.
3. Cover and bake at 350 degrees for 1 hour. Uncover; bake 30-45 minutes longer or until tender. Let stand for 10-15 minutes. Cut into 1/2-in. slices.

Lunch Recipes

Spinach and Lentils

COOKING: 20 MIN

SERVES: 2

INGREDIENTS

1 tablespoon vegetable oil
2 white onions, halved and sliced into 1/2 rings
3 cloves garlic, minced
1/2 cup lentils
2 cups water
1 (10 ounce) package frozen spinach
1 teaspoon salt
1 teaspoon ground cumin freshly ground
Black pepper to taste
2 cloves garlic, crushed

Nutritional Value: 300 calories per serving

DIRECTIONS

1. Heat oil in a heavy pan over medium heat. Sauté onion for 10 minutes or so, until it begins to turn golden. Add minced garlic and sauté for another minute or so.
2. Add lentils and water to the saucepan. Bring mixture to a boil. Cover, lower heat, and simmer about 35 minutes, until lentils are soft (this may take less time, depending on your water and the lentils).
3. Meanwhile cook the spinach in microwave according to package Instructions. Add spinach, salt and cumin to the saucepan. Cover and simmer until all is heated, about ten minutes. Grind in plenty of pepper and press in extra garlic to taste.

Lunch Recipes

 Sandwich with Mushrooms and Artichokes

COOKING: 20 MIN   SERVES: 2

INGREDIENTS

1 (12 inch) French baguettes
1 tablespoon olive oil
12 ounces fresh mushrooms, sliced
1 (14 ounce) can quartered artichoke hearts in water, drained
2 tablespoons grated Parmesan cheese
2 teaspoons garlic and onion seasoning
salt and pepper to taste

Nutritional Value: 478 calories per serving

DIRECTIONS

1. Preheat oven to 350 degrees F (175 degrees C).
2. Slice the baguette in half lengthwise, split open, and toast in the preheated oven until lightly browned, 7 to 9 minutes.
3. Heat the olive oil in a skillet over medium heat, and cook and stir the mushrooms and artichoke hearts until the mushrooms have given up their liquid and have started to brown, about 10 minutes. Stir in the Parmesan cheese, garlic and onion seasoning, and salt and pepper, and cook and stir until the mixture has thickened, about 5 more minutes.
4. Fill the toasted bread with the mushroom filling, close the sandwich, cut in two, and serve.

Lunch Recipes

Stuffed Mushrooms

COOKING: 20 MIN

SERVES: 2

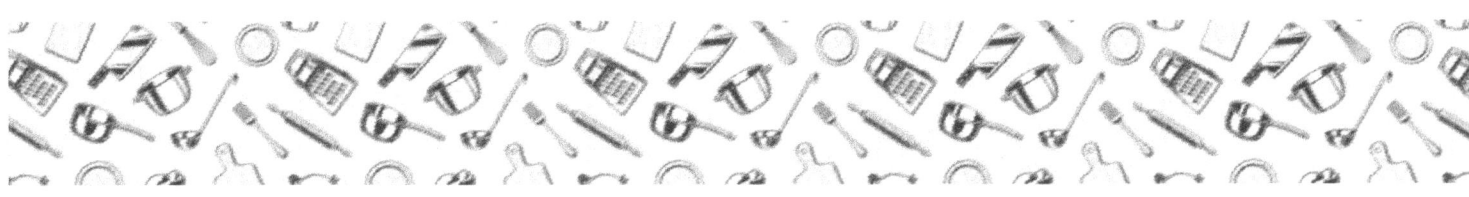

INGREDIENTS

1 cup balsamic vinegar
1/2 teaspoon garlic powder
1/2 teaspoon onion powder
4 large portobello mushrooms, wiped clean and stems removed 2 tablespoons olive oil
1 small eggplant, peeled and diced
1 cup frozen spinach
1/2 cup shredded mozzarella cheese
2 plum tomatoes, diced
1 (6 ounce) jar artichoke hearts in brine, drained and chopped
1/4 cup grated Parmesan cheese

Nutritional Value: 528 calories per serving

DIRECTIONS

1. Stir the balsamic vinegar, garlic powder, and onion powder together in a small bowl until blended. Place the mushrooms into a large resealable plastic bag. Pour in the balsamic vinegar mixture, seal bag, and turn gently to coat mushrooms evenly with marinade.
2. Place in refrigerator for 1 hour.
3. Place the olive oil into a skillet, and heat over medium-high heat. Stir in the eggplant and spinach; cook and stir until eggplant turns golden brown, about 5 minutes.
4. Preheat oven to 350 degrees F (175 degrees C). Lightly grease 9x13 inch baking dish.
5. Remove mushrooms from marinade, shake off any excess, and discard marinade. Place mushrooms in prepared dish, top side down. Spoon the eggplant and spinach mixture evenly over the mushrooms. Sprinkle with mozzarella cheese. Divide the tomatoes and artichoke hearts evenly between the mushrooms. Top each mushroom with Parmesan cheese.
6. Place in preheated oven, and bake until the cheese melts, about 12 minutes. Serve hot.

Lunch Recipes

 **Asparagus Wrapped in Salmon**

COOKING: 20 MIN   SERVES: 2

INGREDIENTS

2 pounds fresh asparagus, trimmed
1 1/2 pounds salmon fillets
1 1/2 cups water
1/2 cup dry white wine or chicken broth
1 tablespoon minced green onion
1 tablespoon minced chives
1 teaspoon salt
1/2 teaspoon whole black peppercorns
Mushroom sauce:
1/2-pound fresh mushrooms, sliced
1/2 cup sliced green onions
2 tablespoons butter or stick margarine
1 teaspoon olive or canola oil
2 tablespoons all-purpose flour
1/2 teaspoon salt
1/8 teaspoon pepper
1 cup 2% milk
1 tablespoon minced chives

Nutritional Value: 455 calories per serving

DIRECTIONS

1. In a large skillet, bring 1/2 in. of water to a boil; add asparagus spears. Reduce heat; cover and simmer for 2 minutes. Drain and immediately place asparagus in ice water; drain and pat dry. Cut salmon widthwise into 1/4-in.-thick slices. To form one bundle, place three to four slices cut side down, overlapping edges slightly; wrap around five to six asparagus spears. Secure with toothpicks. Repeat for remaining bundles.
2. In a large skillet, bring 1-1/2 cups water, wine or broth, onion, chives, salt and peppercorns to a boil. Using a spatula, carefully add bundles. Reduce heat; cover and simmer for 7-8 minutes or until fish flakes easily with a fork.
3. Meanwhile, for sauce, in a skillet, saute mushrooms and green onions in butter and oil until tender. Stir in flour, salt and pepper until blended. Gradually add milk. Bring to a boil; cook and stir for 2 minutes or until thickened. Add chives. Serve over bundles.

Lunch Recipes

Eggplant and Lamb Stew

COOKING: 60+ MIN SERVES: 2

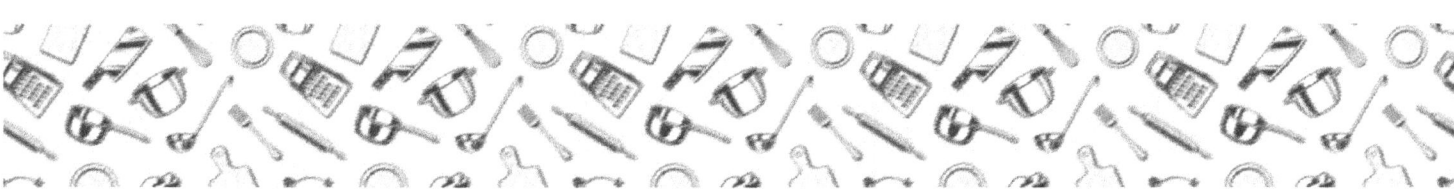

INGREDIENTS

2 tablespoons butter
1 1/2 pounds lamb shoulder
2 large eggplants, peeled and chopped
2 large tomatoes, chopped
2 large onions, chopped
2 green bell peppers, chopped
10 cloves garlic, chopped
1 tablespoon tomato paste
1/2 cup water
1 teaspoon allspice
2 teaspoons salt
1 teaspoon ground black pepper

Nutritional Value: 528 calories per serving

DIRECTIONS

1. In a large pot, melt the butter over medium heat, and brown the lamb on all sides. Mix in the eggplants, tomatoes, onions, green bell peppers, and garlic. Cook and stir until tender and lightly browned.
2. In a small bowl, blend the tomato paste and water. Mix into the pot with the lamb. Season lamb with allspice, salt, and pepper. Reduce heat, and simmer about 1 1/2 hours, stirring occasionally, until the meat shreds easily with a fork. Add a little water as necessary to keep the Ingredients moist.

Lunch Recipes

Burgers with Portobello Mushrooms

COOKING: 50 MIN   SERVES: 2

INGREDIENTS

6 large portobello mushrooms, stems removed
1 eggplant, sliced into 1/2-inch rounds
1 medium yellow squash, slice into 1/4-inch slices
1 zucchini, slice into 1/4-inch slices
1 (16 fl oz) bottle balsamic vinaigrette
1 (4 ounce) package crumbled blue cheese
6 hamburger buns, split and lightly toasted

Nutritional Value: 698 calories per serving

DIRECTIONS

1. Place the mushrooms, eggplant, winter squash, and zucchini into a shallow bowl or baking dish. Drizzle with the balsamic vinaigrette, turning to coat evenly. Cover, and refrigerate at least 2 hours, or up to 24 hours, stirring occasionally.
2. Preheat grill to medium-high heat.
3. Drain vegetables and discard marinade. Place vegetables on preheated grill, and cook until lightly browned, turning once, or about 3 minutes on each side. (Note that cooking times vary between grills.) Sprinkle the mushrooms with blue cheese and let the cheese melt slightly.
4. Open the 6 hamburger buns and divide the eggplant, squash, and zucchini among bottom halves. Place the portobello mushrooms on top of the vegetables, cheese side up. Top with the remaining 6 hamburger bun halves. If necessary, use toothpicks to hold the buns in place. Serve immediately.

Lunch Recipes

Orange Beef and Beans

COOKING: 50 MIN

SERVES: 2

INGREDIENTS

2 tablespoons sugar
1 tablespoon grated orange peel
3/4-pound boneless beef sirloin steak, slice into thin strips
1 tablespoon canola oil
3 cups fresh green beans, slice into 2-inch pieces
2 tablespoons water
1 teaspoon cornstarch
1 teaspoon ground ginger
1/8 teaspoon pepper
1/4 cup reduced-sodium soy sauce
3 tablespoons orange juice

DIRECTIONS

1. In a large bowl, mix sugar and orange peel; mix well. Add beef; toss to coat. In a large nonstick skillet, stir-fry beef in oil for 5 minutes or until browned. In a microwave-safe dish, cover and cook beans in water for 3-5 minutes on high; drain. Add beans to skillet; cook, stirring constantly, until tender.
2. In a bowl, Mix the cornstarch, ginger and pepper. stir in the soy sauce and orange juice until smooth. Pour the sauce over beef and beans; toss to coat. Bring to a boil; cook and stir for 2 minute or until thickened. Serve immediately.

Nutritional Value:

245 calories per serving

Lunch Recipes

Chicken with Cranberry

COOKING: 50 MIN   SERVES: 2

INGREDIENTS

1 tablespoon olive oil
4 skinless, boneless chicken breast halves
1/4 cup orange juice
1/4 cup cranberry juice
1 (10.75 ounce) can condensed Cream of Mushroom Soup
1 tablespoon dried cranberries
1 tablespoon chopped fresh sage leaves
1/8 teaspoon ground black pepper
4 cups hot cooked instant white rice
Sliced green onion

Nutritional Value: 452 calories per serving

DIRECTIONS

1. Heat the oil in a 10-inch skillet over medium-high heat. Add the chicken and cook for 10 minutes or until it's well browned on both sides.
2. Add the orange juice, cranberry juice, soup, cranberries, sage and black pepper in the skillet and heat to a boil. Reduce the heat to low. Cover and cook for 5 minutes or until the chicken is cooked through.
3. Serve the chicken mixture over the rice and sprinkle with the onions.

Lunch Recipes

Penne with Eggplant

COOKING: 50 MIN

SERVES: 2

INGREDIENTS

1 (8 ounce) package penne pasta
2 tablespoons olive oil
1 eggplant, halved lengthwise and slice into small pieces
3 cloves garlic, chopped
2 tablespoons olive oil, or more if needed
salt and pepper to taste
1/4 cup sun-dried tomato spread
1 cup tomato sauce, or more if needed
4 leaves chopped fresh basil

Nutritional Value: 466 calories per serving

DIRECTIONS

1. Fill a large pot with lightly salted water and bring to a rolling boil over high heat. Once the water is boiling, stir in the penne, and return to a boil.
2. Cook the pasta uncovered, stirring occasionally, until the pasta has cooked through, but is still firm to the bite, about 11 minutes.
3. Drain well in a colander set in the sink, reserving 1 cup pasta water.
4. Heat 2 tablespoons olive oil in a large skillet over medium heat. Stir in eggplant and garlic, and drizzle with remaining olive oil to coat; cook and stir until the eggplant is tender and lightly browned, 5 to 7 minutes.
5. Season with salt and pepper.
6. Stir in the sun-dried tomato spread and tomato sauce; cook and stir until heated, through about 5 minutes more.
7. Add penne and toss. Stir in pasta water if the sauce is too thick.
8. Sprinkle with basil before serving.

Lunch Recipes

Eggplant and Mushroom with Wild Rice

COOKING: 50 MIN   SERVES: 2

INGREDIENTS

3 tablespoons butter
3 tablespoons olive oil, divided
1 large eggplant, peeled and cubed
1 medium onion, chopped
8 ounces fresh mushrooms, sliced
1/2 teaspoon minced garlic
1/2 teaspoon salt
1/4 teaspoon ground black pepper
1 teaspoon Italian seasoning
1 cup chicken broth
1 (10.75 ounce) can condensed cream of mushroom soup
1/2 cup half-and-half or light cream
1 cup cooked wild rice

Nutritional Value: 528 calories per serving

DIRECTIONS

1. Heat butter and 1 tablespoon of olive oil in a large skillet. Add the eggplant, and fry until tender, about 5 minutes. Remove eggplant from the skillet and keep warm.
2. Add the remaining 2 tablespoons of olive oil to the skillet, and fry the onion and mushrooms until tender, about 5 minutes. Return the eggplant to the pan, and season with garlic, salt, pepper, and Italian seasoning. Cook and stir for one minute to blend the flavors.
3. Stir in the chicken broth, and simmer for about 5 minutes, until most of the liquid is reduced or absorbed.
4. Stir in cream of mushroom soup, half-and-half cream, and cooked wild rice.
5. Simmer over low heat for 15 minutes, stirring occasionally. Taste and adjust seasoning with salt and pepper if desired.

Lunch Recipes

Eggplant Moussaka

COOKING: 50 MIN   SERVES: 2

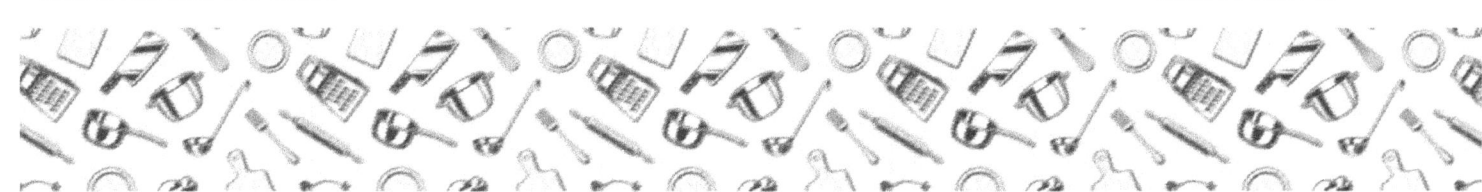

INGREDIENTS

3 large eggplant, sliced into 1/4-inch rounds
3 large potatoes, thinly sliced
3 large zucchinis, slice lengthwise into
1/4-inch slices
1/2 cup extra-virgin olive oil
5 tablespoons butter
7 tablespoons all-purpose flour
5 cups milk
1 pinch ground nutmeg salt to taste
1 egg yolk, beaten
1 tablespoon olive oil
1 1/2 pounds ground beef
1 onion, chopped
1 teaspoon oregano salt and pepper to taste
1/2 cup chopped fresh parsley
5 ripe tomatoes, chopped
1 cup crumbled feta cheese

Nutritional Value: 599 calories per serving

DIRECTIONS

1. Preheat an outdoor grill for medium-high heat and lightly oil grate.
2. Brush eggplant, potatoes, and zucchini lightly with extra-virgin olive oil. Grill vegetables until just tender and golden brown. Layer potatoes into the bottom of a 9x13 inch glass baking dish. Next layer in the eggplant, followed by the zucchini; set aside.
3. Preheat oven to 375 degrees F (190 degrees C).
4. Melt butter in a large saucepan over medium heat. Whisk in the flour, and cook until the flour smells slightly toasted, about 5 minutes. Whisk in milk, nutmeg, and salt. Bring to a bare simmer over medium-high heat, then reduce heat to medium-low and simmer 10 minutes. Place the egg yolk into a bowl, and quickly whisk in 1/4 cup of the thickened milk, a tablespoon at a time.
5. Quickly stir the egg yolk mixture into the thickened milk until smooth, then set aside.
6. Meanwhile, heat 1 tablespoon of olive oil in a large skillet over medium-high heat. Stir in the ground beef and onion and cook until the beef is crumbly and no longer pink. Drain off any excess grease, then stir in the oregano, parsley, tomatoes, salt, and pepper. Turn heat to medium-low, cover, and simmer for 10 minutes, stirring occasionally.
7. To assemble, spread the meat mixture over the vegetables, and sprinkle with the feta cheese. Pour the white sauce over top, and smooth with a spatula.
8. Bake moussaka in preheated oven until bubbly and golden brown, about 30 minutes.

Lunch Recipes

Eggplant Balls

COOKING: 50 MIN   SERVES: 2

INGREDIENTS

3 tablespoons olive oil
3 cloves garlic, minced
4 cups cubed eggplant, with peel
1 tablespoon water
1/2 cup grated Parmesan cheese
1 cup chopped fresh parsley
2 eggs, beaten
3/4 cup dried breadcrumbs

Nutritional Value: 421 calories per serving

DIRECTIONS

1. Preheat oven to 350 degrees F (175 degrees C). Grease a baking sheet.
2. Heat a medium skillet over medium heat. Pour in olive oil and saute garlic just until lightly browned. Mix in eggplant and water. Reduce heat to low and cover skillet. Allow eggplant to steam until soft, about 20 minutes. Place eggplant in a large bowl and allow to cool slightly.
3. Mix cheese, parsley, eggs, and breadcrumbs into eggplant. Stir with a wooden spoon or your hands until Ingredients are thoroughly Mixd and mixture can be rolled into balls. Add more breadcrumbs as needed to make mixture workable. Refrigerate mixture for 15 minutes, then roll into balls or form into patties.
4. Place eggplant balls on prepared baking sheet. Bake in preheated oven for 30 minutes. Serve immediately

Lunch Recipes

Asparagus Pasta

COOKING: 20 MIN

SERVES: 2

INGREDIENTS

1 1/2 pounds fresh asparagus, trimmed and cut into 1-inch pieces
1/4 cup chicken broth
1/2-pound fresh mushrooms, sliced
8 ounces angel hair pasta
1 tablespoon olive oil
1/2 teaspoon crushed red pepper
1/2 cup grated Parmesan cheese

Nutritional Value: 312 calories per serving

DIRECTIONS

1. Cook pasta according to package instructions.
2. Heat the olive oil in a nonstick skillet. Saute asparagus in the pan over medium heat for about 3 minutes. Add chicken broth and mushroom slices; cook 3 minutes more.
3. Drain pasta, and transfer to a serving dish. Gently toss pasta with asparagus mixture; sprinkle with Parmesan and crushed red pepper.

Lunch Recipes

Chicken Burgers with Feta Cheese

COOKING: 20 MIN   SERVES: 2

INGREDIENTS

1-pound ground chicken
1/2 cup dry breadcrumbs
1 egg
1 tablespoon lemon juice
2 tablespoons chopped sun-dried tomatoes
1 tablespoon chopped fresh basil
3 teaspoons chopped fresh oregano
salt and pepper to taste
ounces crumbled feta cheese

Nutritional Value: 689 calories per serving

DIRECTIONS

1. Preheat an outdoor grill for medium-high heat, and lightly oil the grate.
2. Mix the chicken, breadcrumbs, egg, lemon juice, sun-dried tomatoes, basil, oregano, salt, and pepper together in a bowl; form the mixture into 5 patties. Divide the feta cheese between the 5 patties; place a portion of the feta cheese atop each patty and fold the chicken mixture around the cheese so that the cheese is in the center.
3. Cook on the preheated grill until no longer pink on the inside and the juices run clear, 5 to 7 minutes per side. An instant-read thermometer inserted into the center should read 165 degrees F (75 degrees C).

Lunch Recipes

Eggplant Burgers

COOKING: 20 MIN   SERVES: 2

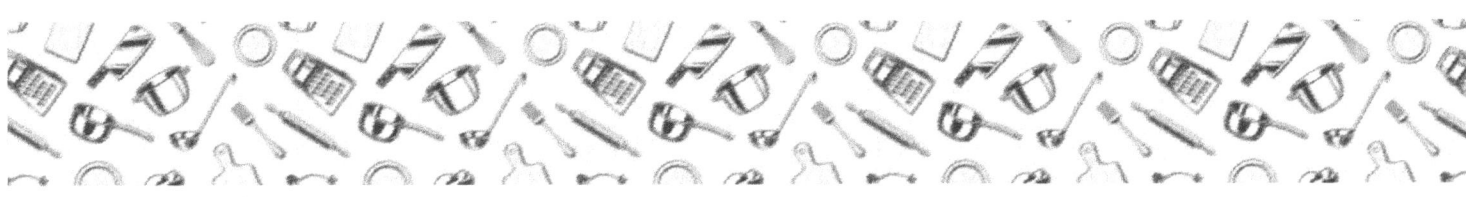

INGREDIENTS

1 eggplant, peeled and sliced into 3/4-inch rounds
1 tablespoon olive oil
6 slices Monterey Jack cheese
6 hamburger buns, split
6 leaves lettuce
6 slices tomato
1/2 onion, sliced
1/2 cup dill pickle slices
1 (20 ounce) bottle ketchup
3 tablespoons mayonnaise
2 tablespoons prepared yellow mustard

Nutritional Value: 247 calories per serving

DIRECTIONS

1. Place the eggplant slices on a plate, and cook in the microwave for about 5 minutes, or until the centers are cooked.
2. Melt olive oil in a large skillet over medium-high heat. Fry eggplant slices until lightly toasted on each side, and place one slice of cheese onto each one. Cook until cheese has melted and remove from the skillet.
3. Place eggplant on hamburger buns, and allow each person to top with lettuce, tomato, onion, and pickles, and dress with ketchup, mayonnaise and mustard.

Lunch Recipes

Rice with Lemon and Spinach

COOKING: 20 MIN   SERVES: 2

INGREDIENTS

1 small onion, chopped
1 cup sliced fresh mushrooms 2 garlic cloves, minced
1 tablespoon olive oil
3 cups cooked long-grain rice
1 (10 ounce) package frozen chopped spinach, thawed and squeezed dry
3 tablespoons lemon juice
1/2 teaspoon salt
1/4 teaspoon dill weed
1/8 teaspoon pepper
1/3 cup crumbled feta cheese, divided

Nutritional Value: 466 calories per serving

DIRECTIONS

1. In a skillet, saute the onion, mushrooms and garlic in oil until tender. Stir in the rice, spinach, lemon juice, salt, dill and pepper. Reserve 1 tablespoon cheese. Stir remaining into skillet; mix well.
2. Transfer to an 8-in. square baking dish coated with nonstick cooking spray. Sprinkle with reserved cheese. Cover and bake at 350 degrees F for 25 minutes. Uncover; bake 5-10 minutes longer or until heated through and cheese is melted.

Lunch Recipes

 Lemon, Parsley and Chicken Breast for Lunch

COOKING: 20 MIN   SERVES: 2

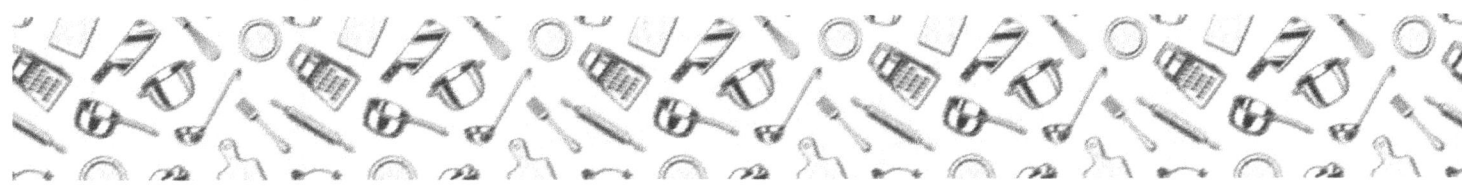

INGREDIENTS

2 whole chicken breasts, boned & skinned
1/3 c. white wine
1/3 c. lemon juice
2 cloves fresh minced garlic
3 tbsp. breadcrumbs
2 tbsp. olive oil
1/4 c. parsley, fresh

Nutritional Value: 478 calories per serving

DIRECTIONS

1. In a measuring cup, combine wine, lemon juice and garlic. Pound each breast until 1/4-inch-thick and lightly coat with breadcrumbs. Heat olive oil in a large skillet and brown chicken, 5 minutes on each side. Stir wine mixture and pour over chicken in skillet. Sprinkle on parsley and let simmer 5 minutes. Serve with pan juices.

Lunch Recipes

 **Black Bean and Artichoke Burritos**

COOKING: 20 MIN   SERVES: 2

INGREDIENTS

1 (15 ounce) can black beans, drained and rinsed
1 tablespoon vegetable oil
1 (10 ounce) can artichoke hearts, drained and sliced
1 medium onion, diced
3 cloves garlic, crushed
8 (10 inch) flour tortillas
2 cups shredded sharp Cheddar cheese
1 large tomato, diced (optional)

Nutritional Value: 477 calories per serving

DIRECTIONS

1. Pour the beans into a large iron skillet and bring to a boil. Cook at a hard simmer until they become pasty and begin to resemble burrito beans in texture.
2. Heat oil in a separate skillet over medium heat. Stir in artichoke hearts, onion, and garlic; cook until the artichokes become golden brown.
3. Place tortillas in a dry skillet over low heat to warm. Remove from skillet. Spoon beans and artichoke mixture onto each tortilla, and top with cheese and tomato. Fold in ends and roll up.

Lunch Recipes

 **Sesame Vegetables with Rice**

COOKING: 20 MIN   SERVES: 2

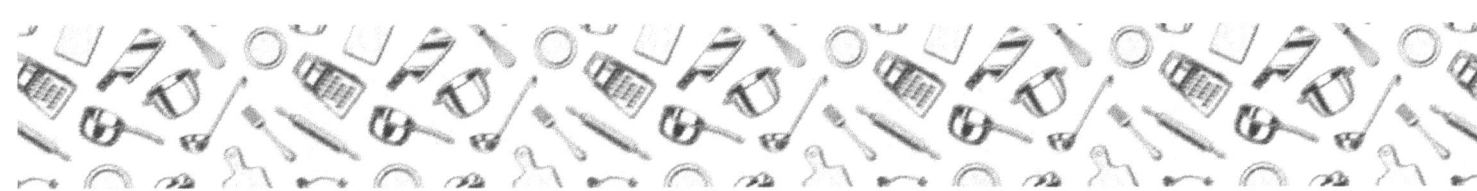

INGREDIENTS

1 1/2 cups vegetable broth
3/4 cup uncooked long-grain white rice
1 tablespoon margarine
1 tablespoon sesame seeds
2 tablespoons peanut oil
1/2-pound fresh asparagus, trimmed and cut into 1-inch pieces
1 large red bell pepper, cut into 1-inch pieces
1 large yellow onion, sliced
2 cups sliced mushrooms
2 teaspoons minced fresh ginger root
1 teaspoon minced garlic 3 tablespoons soy sauce 1 tablespoon sesame oil

Nutritional Value: 333 calories per serving

DIRECTIONS

1. Preheat oven to 350 degrees F (175 degrees C). In a saucepan combine broth, rice and margarine. Cover and bring to a boil over high heat. Reduce heat to low and simmer for 15 minutes, or until all liquid is absorbed.
2. Place sesame seeds on a small baking sheet and bake in preheated oven for 5 to 6 minutes, or until golden brown; set aside.
3. Meanwhile, heat peanut oil in a large skillet or wok over medium-high heat until very hot. Add asparagus, bell pepper, onion, mushrooms, ginger and garlic and stir-fry for 4 to 5 minutes, or until vegetables are tender but crisp. Stir in soy-sauce and cook for 30 seconds. Remove from heat and stir in sesame oil and toasted sesame seeds. Serve over rice.

Lunch Recipes

Syrian Style Lentil and Spinach Soup

COOKING: 20 MIN   SERVES: 2

INGREDIENTS

1 tablespoon olive oil
1 onion, chopped
2/3 cup dry green lentils
1 3/4 cups water
1 tablespoon all-purpose flour
2/3 cup chopped fresh spinach
3 tablespoons lemon juice
1/2 teaspoon salt

Nutritional Value: 528 calories per serving

DIRECTIONS

1. Heat oil in a pot over medium heat. Stir in onion and cook until soft about 7 minutes, stirring occasionally. Add the lentils and water and bring to a boil, then reduce heat to low and simmer, uncovered, until lentils are tender, 20 to 25 minutes. Cooking times will vary depending on the freshness of the lentils.
2. Ladle a half cup of the soup liquid into a bowl and whisk in the flour to form a paste. Mix the paste into the soup. Add the spinach, lemon juice, and salt. If you prefer a thinner soup, add a bit more water. Cook until spinach is wilted, about 5 minutes. Adjust salt and lemon to suit your taste.

Lunch Recipes

 **Roasted Red Potatoes and Asparagus**

COOKING: 20 MIN SERVES: 2

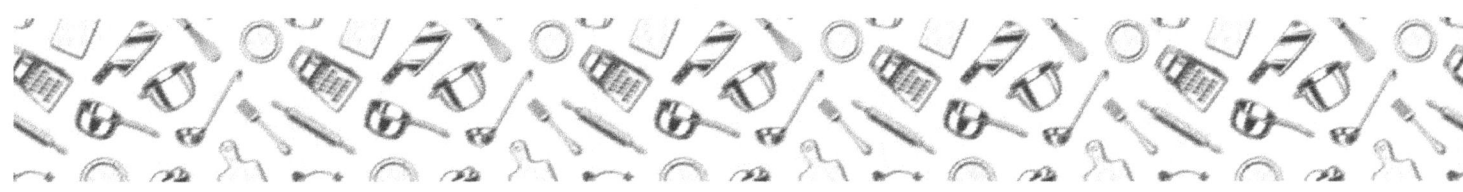

INGREDIENTS

1 1/2 pounds red potatoes, cut into chunks
2 tablespoons extra virgin olive oil
8 cloves garlic, thinly sliced
4 teaspoons dried rosemary
4 teaspoons dried thyme
2 teaspoons kosher salt
1 bunch fresh asparagus, trimmed and cut into 1-inch pieces
ground black pepper to taste

Nutritional Value: 248 calories per serving

DIRECTIONS

1. Preheat oven to 425 degrees F (220 degrees C).
2. In a large baking dish, toss the red potatoes with 1/2 the olive oil, garlic, rosemary, thyme, and 1/2 the kosher salt. Cover with aluminum foil.
3. Bake 20 minutes in the preheated oven. Mix in the asparagus, remaining olive oil, and remaining salt. Cover, and continue cooking 15 minutes, or until the potatoes are tender. Increase oven temperature to 450 degrees F (230 degrees C). Remove foil, and continue cooking 5 to 10 minutes, until potatoes are lightly browned. Season with pepper to serve.

Lunch Recipes

 **Spinach and Rice (It can be used as Brunch)**

COOKING: 20 MIN   SERVES: 2

INGREDIENTS

1/3 cup olive oil
2 onions, chopped
2 pounds fresh spinach, rinsed and stemmed
1 (8 ounce) can tomato sauce
2 cups water
1 teaspoon dried dill weed
1 teaspoon dried parsley salt and pepper to taste
1/2 cup uncooked white rice

Nutritional Value: 257 calories per serving

DIRECTIONS

1. Heat olive oil in a large skillet over medium-high heat. Saute onions in the oil until soft and translucent. Add spinach, and cook stirring for a few minutes, then pour in the tomato sauce and water. Bring to a boil, and season with parsley, dill, salt and pepper. Stir in rice, reduce heat to low, and simmer uncovered for 20 to 25 minutes, or until rice is tender. Add more water if necessary.

Lunch Recipes

 **Sweet Potatoes with Raisins and Pecans**

COOKING: 50 MIN   SERVES: 2

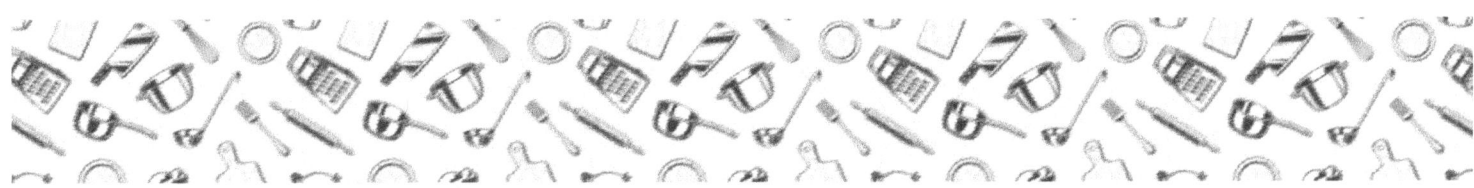

INGREDIENTS

5 sweet potatoes, peeled and cubed
1-ounce raisins
1-ounce chopped pecans
1/4 cup butter, melted
1/2 cup maple syrup
1/2 cup water

Nutritional Value: 528 calories per serving

DIRECTIONS

1. Preheat oven to 400 degrees F (200 degrees C).
2. Spread sweet potatoes in a single layer in a 9x13 inch baking dish. Sprinkle with raisins and chopped pecans.
3. In a small bowl, mix the butter, syrup and water. Pour the mixture over potatoes.
4. Cover the baking dish with aluminum foil. Bake in the preheated oven 50 to 60 minutes, until sweet potatoes are tender.

Lunch Recipes

 **Orange Couscous**

COOKING: 50 MIN   SERVES: 2

INGREDIENTS

1 (10 ounce) box uncooked plain couscous
1 (11 ounce) can mandarin oranges, drained and liquid reserved
1/4 cup pine nuts, lightly toasted

Nutritional Value: 698 calories per serving

DIRECTIONS

1. Prepare the couscous according to package instructions using the drained mandarin orange liquid as part of the specified amount of water. Fluff the couscous, and gently stir in the pine nuts and mandarin oranges. Serve hot.

Lunch Recipes

Chicken with Almonds

COOKING: 50 MIN   SERVES: 10

INGREDIENTS

10 chicken breast halves
Salt and pepper
1 (5 1/2 oz.) pkg. slivered almonds
1 (10 1/2 oz.) can cream of mushroom soup
1 (10 1/2 oz.) can cream of chicken soup
1/4 to 1/2 c. dry white wine, or water or other liquid
Parmesan cheese

Nutritional Value: 457 calories per serving

DIRECTIONS

1. Spread chicken in very lightly greased baking dish.
2. Cover with 2/3 of the almonds. Mix soups with wine.
3. Pour over chicken and almonds.
4. Sprinkle Parmesan cheese on top and then sprinkle remaining almonds over.
5. Bake at 350 degrees for 2 hours uncovered.

Lunch Recipes

Eggplant and Garlic Sauce

COOKING: 50 MIN   SERVES: 2

INGREDIENTS

3 tablespoons canola oil
4 Chinese eggplants, halved lengthwise and slice into 1-inch half moons
1 cup water
1 tablespoon crushed red pepper flakes
3 tablespoons garlic powder
5 teaspoons raw honey
1 teaspoon cornstarch
2 tablespoons light soy sauce
2 tablespoons oyster sauce

Nutritional Value: 258 calories per serving

DIRECTIONS

1. Heat the canola oil in a skillet over high heat. Cook and stir the eggplant until soft, about 4 minutes. Stir in the water, red pepper flakes, and garlic powder. Cover and simmer until all the water is absorbed.
2. Meanwhile, mix sugar, cornstarch, soy sauce, and oyster sauce in a bowl until sugar and cornstarch have dissolved. Stir sauce into the eggplant, making sure to evenly coat the eggplant.
3. Cook until the sauce has thickened.

Dinner Recipes

Orange Lamb

COOKING: 35 MIN

SERVES: 4

INGREDIENTS

1 large orange, juiced
3 tablespoons dark French mustard
tablespoons olive oil
teaspoons dried oregano salt and pepper to taste
10 potatoes, peeled and slice into 2-inch pieces
1 (3 pound) half leg of lamb, bone-in
5 cloves garlic

Nutritional Value: 336 calories per serving

DIRECTIONS

1. Preheat oven to 375 degrees F (190 degrees C).
2. In large bowl, whisk together the orange juice, mustard, olive oil, oregano, salt, and pepper. Stir the potatoes into the bowl to coat with orange juice mixture. Remove potatoes with a slotted spoon and place them into a large roasting pan.
3. Slice slits into the lamb meat, and stuff the garlic cloves into the slits. Rub remaining orange juice mixture from bowl all over the lamb and place the lamb on top of the potatoes in the roasting pan. If there's any remaining orange juice mixture, pour it over the lamb.
4. Roast in the preheated oven until the potatoes are tender and the lamb is cooked to medium, about 1 hour. A meat thermometer inserted into the thickest part of the meat should read 140 degrees F (60 degrees C). Check every 20 to 30 minutes while roasting and add a bit of hot water if you find the potatoes are drying out. If the lamb finishes cooking before the potatoes, remove the lamb to a slicing board or serving platter and cover with foil while the potatoes continue to bake in the oven.

Dinner Recipes

Spinach and Turkey Lasagna

COOKING: 35 MIN   SERVES: 4

INGREDIENTS

9 whole-wheat lasagna noodles
1 teaspoon olive oil
1/2 cup chopped onion
1-pound ground turkey breast
3 cups tomato sauce
1/2 cup sliced fresh mushrooms
3 tablespoons Italian seasoning
1/4 teaspoon ground black pepper
1/4 teaspoon garlic powder
6 cups chopped fresh spinach
2 cups fat-free ricotta cheese
1/4 teaspoon ground nutmeg
2 cups shredded mozzarella cheese

Nutritional Value: 488 calories per serving

DIRECTIONS

1. Preheat an oven to 375 degrees F (190 degrees C).
2. Bring a large pot of lightly salted water to a boil. Cook lasagna noodles in boiling water for 8 to 10 minutes. Drain noodles, and rinse with cold water.
3. Heat the olive oil in a skillet over medium heat. Stir in the onion; cook and stir until the onion has softened and turned translucent, about 2 minutes. Add ground turkey and cook 5 to 7 minutes more, stirring to break up any large chunks of meat. Stir in tomato sauce, mushrooms, Italian seasoning, black pepper, and garlic powder.
4. Simmer for 2 minutes and season to taste.
5. Combine spinach, ricotta, and nutmeg in a large bowl.
6. To assemble, arrange 3 noodles lengthwise in the bottom of a greased 9x13 inch baking dish. Spread with 1/3 the ricotta mixture, 1/3 of the turkey mixture, and 1/3 of the mozzarella. Repeat layers, ending with remaining mozzarella. Bake in preheated oven for 25 minutes. Cool for 5 minutes before serving.

Dinner Recipes

Steak and Potato Salad

COOKING: 35 MIN

SERVES: 4

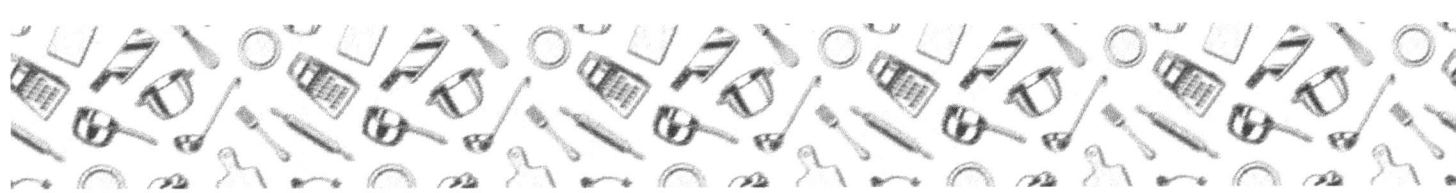

INGREDIENTS

1/4 cup red wine vinegar
1 tablespoon Dijon mustard
2 teaspoons jarred minced garlic
1 teaspoon salt
1/2 teaspoon dried thyme leaves
1/2 teaspoon freshly ground black pepper
1/2 teaspoon granulated raw honey
3/4 cup oil
1 1/2 pounds small red potatoes, scrubbed and quartered
1-pound boneless sirloin, New York Strip or Delmonico steak
1/2-pound fresh green beans, slice into 1-inch pieces
1/2-pound white mushrooms, rinsed, stems trimmed and thinly sliced
1 medium red bell pepper, seeds and ribs removed and thinly sliced
1/2 small red onion, peeled and thinly sliced
1-pint cherry tomatoes, rinsed and halved
Bibb or head lettuce leaves

Nutritional Value: 322 calories per serving

DIRECTIONS

1. Whisk together vinegar, mustard, garlic, salt, thyme, pepper and raw honey. Add oil; whisk until thoroughly blended.
2. Place steak in re-sealable plastic bag. Pour one-third of dressing over meat. Marinate 30 minutes.
3. Place potatoes in large pot. Cover with cold water; add salt. Bring to boil on high heat. Boil for 12-15 minutes, or until tender when pierced with a knife. Drain. Place in large mixing bowl. Toss with half of remaining dressing.
4. Prepare grill or broiler.
5. Microwave green beans on high for 2 minutes, or until crisp-tender. Set aside. Add green beans, mushrooms, red bell pepper, onion and tomatoes to potatoes; toss gently to mix.
6. Remove steak from marinade, discard marinade. Season steak with salt and pepper.
7. Grill steak to desired doneness; allow to rest 5 minutes before slicing into thin slices across the grain.
8. Arrange lettuce leaves on 4 plates. Top with vegetable mixture. Place steak slices on top; drizzle with remaining dressing. Serve immediately.

Dinner Recipes

Filled Tomatoes

COOKING: 35 MIN

SERVES: 4

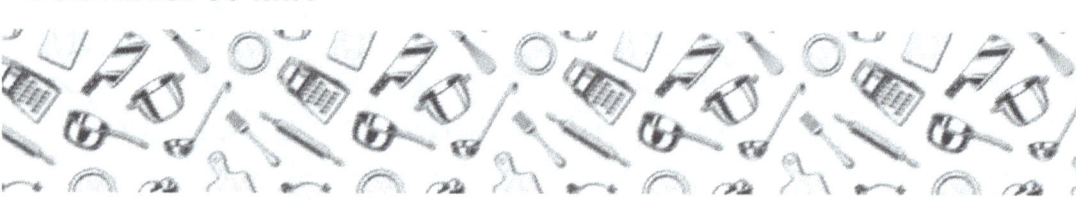

INGREDIENTS

4 large ripe tomatoes salt and pepper to taste
1 tablespoon olive oil
1 cucumber, peeled and diced
1/2 cup yogurt
8 ounces black Greek olives, pitted and sliced
1/4 cup chopped fresh basil
1 teaspoon raw honey
2 cups crumbled feta cheese
1/4 cup chopped fresh parsley

Nutritional Value: 293 calories per serving

DIRECTIONS

1. Preheat oven to 350 degrees F (175 degrees C).
2. Slice tomatoes in half, scoop out seeds, and place in a baking dish sliced side up. Sprinkle with and salt and pepper. Bake for 5 minutes. Remove tomatoes from oven, drizzle with olive oil, and bake an additional 10 minutes.
3. While baking tomatoes, mix together cucumber, yogurt, olives, basil, and raw honey. Stir in feta cheese. Season to taste with salt and pepper.
4. Remove tomatoes from oven, fill with cucumber mixture, and sprinkle with parsley. Serve immediately.

Dinner Recipes

Greek Lamb Roast

COOKING: 50 MIN

SERVES: 4

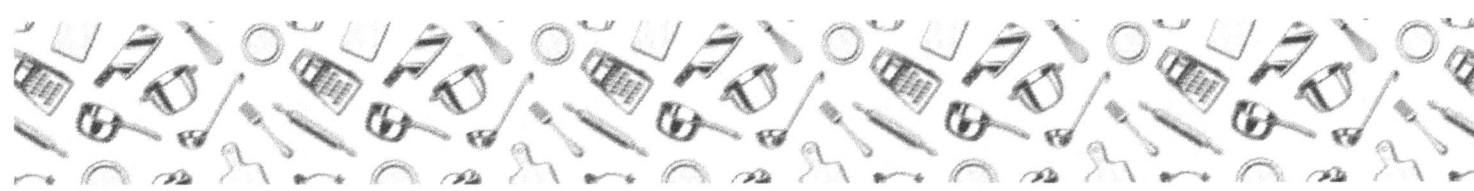

INGREDIENTS

1 large orange, juiced
3 tablespoons dark French mustard
3 tablespoons olive oil
4 teaspoons dried oregano salt and pepper to taste
10 potatoes, peeled and slice into 2-inch pieces
1 (3 pound) half leg of lamb, bone-in
5 cloves garlic

Nutritional Value: 291 calories per serving

DIRECTIONS

1. Preheat oven to 375 degrees F (190 degrees C).
2. In large bowl, whisk together the orange juice, mustard, olive oil, oregano, salt, and pepper. Stir the potatoes into the bowl to coat with orange juice mixture. Remove potatoes with a slotted spoon and place them into a large roasting pan.
3. Slice slits into the lamb meat, and stuff the garlic cloves into the slits. Rub remaining orange juice mixture from bowl all over the lamb and place the lamb on top of the potatoes in the roasting pan. If there's any remaining orange juice mixture, pour it over the lamb.
4. Roast in the preheated oven until the potatoes are tender and the lamb is cooked to medium, about 1 hour. A meat thermometer inserted into the thickest part of the meat should read 140 degrees F (60 degrees C). Check every 20 to 30 minutes while roasting and add a bit of hot water if you find the potatoes are drying out. If the lamb finishes cooking before the potatoes, remove the lamb to a slicing board or serving platter and cover with foil while the potatoes continue to bake in the oven.

Dinner Recipes

 Keftedes

COOKING: 40 MIN   SERVES: 4

INGREDIENTS

Oil for frying
1/4 cup fresh lemon juice
5 white potatoes, peeled 2 pounds ground beef
1 large onion, grated
3/4 cup dry breadcrumbs
cup chopped fresh parsley
1/3 cup dried mint, crushed
1/2 teaspoon ground cinnamon zest from
1 lemon
2 eggs, beaten
1 1/2 tablespoons salt
1 teaspoon ground black pepper
lemon wedges

Nutritional Value: 291 calories per serving

DIRECTIONS

1. Heat oil in a deep-fryer or large saucepan to 325 degrees F (165 degrees C).
2. Place the lemon juice in a large bowl. Coarsely grate the potatoes into the lemon juice, stirring well to prevent browning. Stir in the ground beef, onion, breadcrumbs, parsley, mint, cinnamon, lemon zest, eggs, and salt and pepper. Mix well, and shape into oblong balls about 1 inch thick and 2 inches wide.
3. Place meatballs in hot oil in batches; do not crowd. Fry until golden brown, and cooked through, about 6 to 7 minutes per batch. Serve with lemon wedges.

Dinner Recipes

Turkey with Pine and Chestnuts

COOKING: 35 MIN

SERVES: 4

INGREDIENTS

1 cup chestnuts
2/3 cup butter
1/4 cup orange juice
1/4 cup tangerine juice
2/3 cup lemon juice
1 (10 pound) whole turkey
salt and ground black pepper to taste
1/2-pound ground beef
1/2-pound ground pork
1/4 cup chopped onion
1/2 cup uncooked instant rice
1/4 cup pine nuts
1/4 cup raisins (optional)
1/3 cup butter
1/2 cup chicken broth
\2 tablespoons brandy
1 teaspoon salt
1/2 teaspoon ground black pepper

Nutritional Value: 258 calories per serving

DIRECTIONS

1. Preheat oven to 325 degrees F (165 degrees C).
2. Make a small incision on sides of each chestnut, and place in a skillet over medium heat. Cook, stirring often, until toasted. Remove from heat, peel, and chop.
3. Melt 2/3 cup butter in a saucepan, and mix in the orange juice, tangerine juice, and lemon juice. Rub the turkey inside and out with the mixture, reserving some for basting. Season turkey with salt and pepper.
4. In a large skillet over medium heat, cook the ground beef, ground pork, and onion until beef and pork are evenly brown and onion is tender. Drain grease. Mix in the rice. Stir in the chestnuts, pine nuts, raisins, 1/3 cup butter, broth, and brandy. Season with 1 teaspoon salt and 1/2 teaspoon pepper. Continue cooking until all liquid has been absorbed. Stuff all turkey cavities with the mixture, and tie in place with kitchen twine.
5. Place turkey on a rack in a roasting pan, and loosely cover breast and thighs with aluminum foil. Pour about 1/4-inch water into the bottom of the pan. Maintain this level of water throughout cook time. Roast turkey in the preheated oven 3 to 4 hours, brushing occasionally with remaining butter and juice mixture. Increase oven temperature to 400 degrees F (200 degrees C) during final hour of roasting and remove foil. Cook turkey to a minimum internal temperature of 180 degrees F (82 degrees C).

Dinner Recipes

Stuffed Peppers

COOKING: 35 MIN

SERVES: 4

INGREDIENTS

1/2-pound orzo pasta
2 tablespoons olive oil
1 yellow onion, chopped
large cloves garlic, chopped 1
1/2 pounds ground lamb
4 1/2 teaspoons dried oregano
1 tablespoon dried basil
salt and pepper to taste
(16 ounce) package frozen chopped spinach, thawed and drained
tomatoes, diced
1 (6 ounce) can tomato paste
8 ounces crumbled feta cheese
6 large green or red bell peppers - tops removed and seeded
olive oil

Nutritional Value: 325 calories per serving

DIRECTIONS

1. Bring a pot of lightly salted water to a boil over high heat. Cook the orzo in the boiling water uncovered, stirring occasionally, until tender yet firm to the bite, about 8 minutes. Drain.
2. Heat 2 tablespoons olive oil in a large skillet over medium high heat; cook and stir the onion and garlic in the hot oil until fragrant, about 1 minute. Crumble the ground lamb into the mixture; season with the oregano, basil, and salt and pepper. Continue cooking until the lamb is completely browned, 7 to 10 minutes. Remove from heat.
3. Stir the orzo, spinach, tomatoes, tomato paste, and feta cheese into the lamb mixture until evenly incorporated.
4. Evenly rub the outside of the bell peppers and the tops with 2 tablespoons olive oil. Season with salt and pepper. Arrange in a baking dish large enough to accommodate all of them standing upright. Fill the peppers with the lamb mixture and replace the tops.
5. Roast in the preheated oven until the peppers begin to brown, 30 to 40 minutes.

Dinner Recipes

Crab Cakes

COOKING: 20 MIN   SERVES: 4

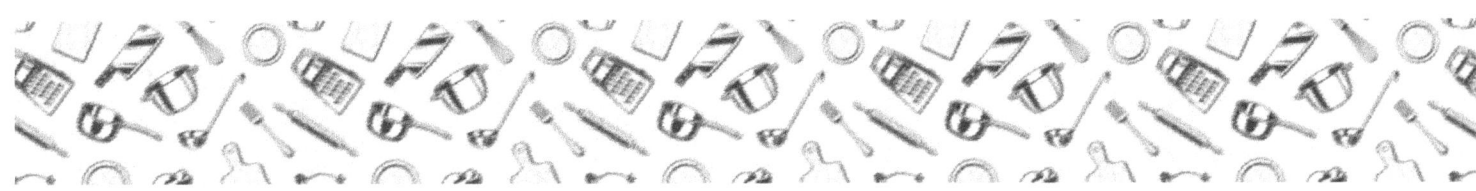

INGREDIENTS

8 oz crabmeat
1.5 cup whole grain breadcrumbs
1 egg
4 teaspoon lemon juice
1.5 teaspoon salt
1.5 teaspoon dried oregano herbs
270
3-4 fresh basil leaves, finely chopped
1.5 teaspoon chili flakes
1.5 teaspoon black pepper
2 tbsp olive oil
1.25 cup onion, finely minced

Nutritional Value: 300 calories per serving

DIRECTIONS

1. Mix together the egg, oregano, basil, onion, lemon juice, and the crabmeat. Gently stir and gradually incorporate the breadcrumbs so the mixture becomes to the desired texture. Form the mixture into 4 evenly sized round patties using the palms of your hands. (If your hands become sticky from the mixture, apply a few drops of olive oil to help you handle the meat.) In a small pan, add your olive oil and fry your crab cakes on both sides until they are cooked through and golden in color. Now that you have them made, you can eat them with quinoa, rice, or add to a healthy salad for a delicious source of protein.

Dinner Recipes

 **Lentil Soup**

COOKING: 20 MIN   SERVES: 4

INGREDIENTS

1.5 onion, chopped
1.5 cup carrots, chopped
3 tbsp olive oil
1 bay leaf
1 tablespoon vinegar
1.5 cup celery, chopped
2 teaspoon garlic, minced
1.5 teaspoon dried oregano
1 cup dry lentils
1.5 teaspoon salt
2 tomatoes, chopped 271
4 cups of water
1.5 teaspoon dried basil
1.5 cup spinach, chopped
1.5 teaspoon black pepper

Nutritional Value: 258 calories per serving

DIRECTIONS

1. Add the olive oil to a large pot and sauté your celery, onions, and carrots until the veggies become soft. Next, add your dried herbs, the bay leaf, and the minced garlic and stir until everything is well Mixd with the herbs. Then add the lentils, water, and tomatoes. In order to cook your lentils, raise the heat then let the mixture simmer for 15 to 20 minutes. Stir in your spinach and when it wilts, you can turn off the heat and add your seasoning (vinegar, salt, and black pepper.

Dinner Recipes

Greek Tacos

COOKING: 35 MIN   SERVES: 4

INGREDIENTS

2 cups chicken
1 cup olives
4 cups Romanian lettuce
1 cup tomatoes
1.75 cup cucumber
1 cup cilantro
1 cup feta cheese
1 cup Greek dressing
1 cup dill dip
8 tortillas

Nutritional Value:

466 calories per serving

DIRECTIONS

1. Do the preparation. Grill the chicken to your liking. Shred the lettuce and slice the black olives. Dice the tomatoes, cucumbers, and cilantro. Crumble the feta cheese and set aside.
2. Mix all of the fixings except for the tortilla, dip, dressing, and cheese.
3. Warm up the tortilla. Fill with the salad. Garnish with the dip and feta cheese.
4. Serve right way.

Dinner Recipes

Mussels with Potatoes and Black Olives

COOKING: 30 MIN

SERVES: 4

INGREDIENTS

2 lb. mussels
2 potatoes
14 oz tomatoes, diced
1 onion, sliced
1 cup black olives
2 teaspoons minced garlic
1 teaspoon cayenne pepper
1 tablespoon salt
1 tablespoon paprika
1 teaspoon parsley
Olive oil
Water

Nutritional Value: 345 calories per serving

DIRECTIONS

1. Peel the potatoes and slice into 1-inch cubes. Add to a pot of water, covering the potatoes with ¼-inch of water. Cover with plastic wrap.
2. Place in the microwave for 6 minutes using the high heat setting.
3. Prepare a large pot using the medium-high heat setting. Pour in the oil. When hot, toss in the garlic and onion. Simmer for 6 minutes.
4. Drain the potatoes and add to the cooker. Sprinkle with the allspice, paprika, pepper, and salt.
5. Stir well and simmer for 2 to 3 minutes. Pour in the tomatoes and water. Stir to remove the delicious brown bits from the bottom of the cooker.
6. Lastly, add the parsley, olives, and mussels. Simmer for 5 more minutes with a lid on. Serve immediately.

Dinner Recipes

 Skewers from Lemon and Chicken

COOKING: 20 MIN   SERVES: 6

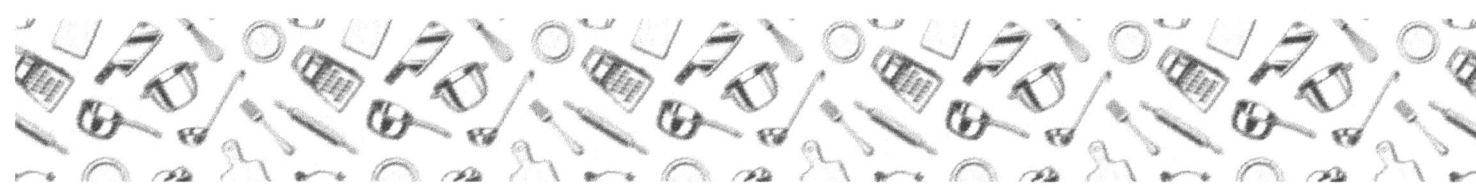

INGREDIENTS

1.25 cup olive oil
3 tbsp. lemon juice
1 tablespoon white vinegar
2 teaspoons lemon zest
1 teaspoon salt
1.25 dried oregano
1 black pepper
Raw Honey
3 zucchinis
2 garlic cloves
1 onion
12 cherry tomatoes
1.5 lb. chicken breasts

Nutritional Value: 219 calories per serving

DIRECTIONS

1. Slice the zucchini in half lengthwise and slice into 1.5-inch slices.
2. Peel the onions and slice into wedges. Zest the lemon. Slice the chicken into 1.5-inch pieces.
3. Prepare the marinade; Mix the raw honey, pepper, oregano, salt, lemon zest, vinegar, lemon juice, and oil - reserving .25 cup for basting.
4. Fold in the chicken and toss to cover.
5. Add the rest of the marinade in a mixing container and add the tomatoes, onions, and zucchini. Cover and place in the fridge overnight (for best results) or a minimum of four hours.
6. When ready to cook, drain and trash the marinade.
7. Soak the wooden skewers in water.
8. Thread the chicken and veggies onto the soaked skewers.
9. Place the skewers on the grill for six minutes using the medium heat setting. It's done when poked with a fork - the juices will run clear.

Dinner Recipes

 **Spinach and Cherries with Goat Cheese**

COOKING: 35 MIN   SERVES: 2

INGREDIENTS

1 tablespoon olive oil
2 cloves garlic, minced
1 small onion, chopped
1/4 cup dried cherries
1 cup sliced fresh mushrooms
1 (10 ounce) bag fresh baby spinach
2 tablespoons crumbled goat cheese

Nutritional Value: 220 calories per serving

DIRECTIONS

1. Heat olive oil in a large skillet over very low heat. Add garlic, onion, cherries, and mushrooms; cook and stir, without browning garlic, until onion is tender, about 5 minutes. Toss in spinach, and cook and stir until spinach is just wilted, about 3 minutes.
2. Remove from heat. Top with crumbled goat cheese just before serving.

Dinner Recipes

Eggplant and Tomato Bake

COOKING: 35 MIN

SERVES: 2

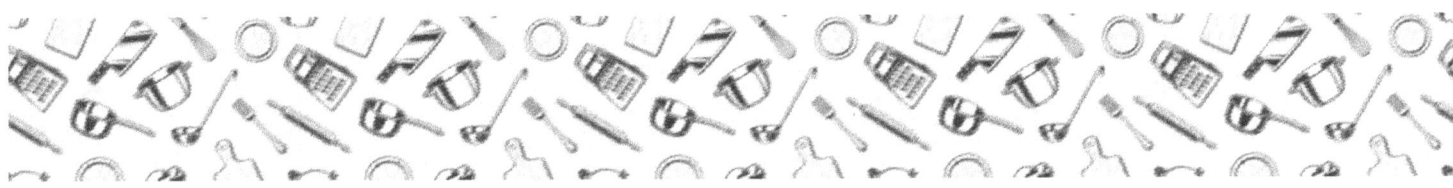

INGREDIENTS

2-3 eggplants
3 tsp. salt
1/4 cup flour
2/3 cup oil
2 onions, chopped
18 oz. can tomatoes
1 tsp. dried basil
1/2 tsp. oregano, dried
1 tsp. sugar
1/4 tsp. black pepper
8 oz. mozzarella cheese
1/4 cup parmesan cheese
1/4 cup tomato paste

Nutritional Value: 330 calories per serving

DIRECTIONS

1. Slice eggplants into 1/2" slices; sprinkle with 2 tsp. salt.
2. Roll slices, moistened, in flour. Fry slices in heated oil, in skillet until brown on each side. Drain. Add onions, tomatoes,
3. remaining salt, tomato paste, basil, oregano, sugar and pepper to oil remaining in skillet and cook 10 minutes. Cool slightly, bend mixture or push through strainer. Place half the mixture in greased baking dish. Add a layer of eggplant slices and a layer of cheese slices. Top with remaining tomato mixture and sprinkle top with cheese. Bake at 400 degrees for 20 minutes.

Dinner Recipes

Mediterranean Veggie Chicken

COOKING: 35 MIN

SERVES: 2

INGREDIENTS

1 teaspoon of Himalayan salt or regular salt,
1 teaspoon black pepper
1 teaspoon paprika
3 green onions, chopped
2 large boneless skinless chicken breasts
2-3 tomatoes, diced
2 small jalapeno peppers, de-seeded and thinly sliced
2 tbsp lemon juice
1 bell pepper, chopped

Nutritional Value: 291 calories per serving

DIRECTIONS

1. Mix your lemon juice with spices and use the mixture to season your chicken breasts. On a lined baking tray, place your chicken breasts and chopped vegetables. Bake for 30 to 35 minutes at 450 degrees F covered with foil to trap the moisture. Once cooked, you can broil it for a few minutes to add more color to your chicken.

30-day meal plan

	Breakfast	**Lunch**	**Dinner**
Day 1	Spicy Biscotti with Raspberry Jam	Tomato Cucumber and Onion Salad	Chicken Spinach Salad
Day 2	Strawberry R. Smoothie	Spinach Noodles	Tuna Salad with Oranges
Day 3	Seafood Omelet	Black Bean Chili	Quick Bread with Orange
Day 4	Spinach Pancakes	Cold Rice Salad	Chicken Stew
Day 5	French Toast with Pecans	Eggplant Yogurt Salad	Pear Salad
Day 6	Polenta Cake	Artichoke Soup with Oysters	Tomato and Eggplant Soup
Day 7	Scrambled Eggs from Greece	Spinach Peaches and Pecan Salad	Bread with Pears
Day 8	Mango Pear Smoothie	Anna's Salad	Tomato Cucumber and Onion Salad
Day 9	Avocado Stuffed	Chickpea, Garlic, Spinach Soup	The Perfect Italian Bread with Dressing by choice
Day 10	Oven Omelet with Pears	Spring Soup	Chickpea, Garlic, Spinach Soup
Day 11	Lemon and Strawberry Smoothie	Chicken Stew	Onion Garlic Bread
Day 12	Scalloped Eggs	Cabbage Onion and Tomato Salad	Spring Soup
Day 13	Orange Pancakes	Ranch Salad	Creamy Orange Rice Salad
Day 14	Oatmeal Smoothie	Pasta Bake with Vegetables and Cheese	Cold Rice Salad
Day 15	Italian Cheese Toast	Shrimp Pasta with Feta Cheese	Pepper Salad
Day 16	Nectarine Smoothie	Tomato and Eggplant Soup	Spinach and Feta Pasta

Day 17	Italian Sandwich for Breakfast	Quinoa and Lentil Salad	Olive Orange Chicken Cutlets
Day 18	Triple Fruit Smoothie	Chicken with Mushrooms and Tomatoes	Chicken Stew
Day 19	Oatmeal Apricot Bites	Lamb Chops with Mint	Casserole from Pasta and Beans
Day 20	Banana Pineapple Smoothie	Chickpea, Garlic, Spinach Soup	Mediterranean Broccoli Salad
Day 21	Avocado and Egg Sandwich	Greek Pita Pizzas	Spinach, Peaches and Pecan Salad
Day 22	Potato Pancakes	Chicken Stew	Bean Salad
Day 23	Scrambled Eggs with Shrimps	Onion Salmon	Ham and Sea Spaghetti
Day 24		Chicken Cutlets	Tuna Casserole
Day 25	Orange Coconut Smoothie	Tomato Spinach Pizza	Chicken Stew
Day 26	Scalloped Eggs	4th of July Pasta	Steak with Vegetable and Salsa
Day 27	Spinach Pancakes	Tomato Cucumber and Onion Salad	Spring Soup
Day 28	Apple Smoothie	Quail with Pomegranate	Chickpea, Garlic, Spinach Soup
Day 29	Terrine for Breakfast	Black Bean and Spinach Pizza	Tomato Octopus
Day 30	Peach Cinnamon Smoothie	Chickpea, Garlic, Spinach Soup	Peperonata Steak

www.ingramcontent.com/pod-product-compliance
Lightning Source LLC
Chambersburg PA
CBHW081338080526
44588CB00017B/2660